THE SPIRIT: THE MOVIE VISUAL COMPANION
ISBN: 9781845768324

Published by
Titan Books
A division of
Titan Publishing Group Ltd
144 Southwark St
London
SE1 0UP

First edition November 2008
10 9 8 7 6 5 4 3 2 1

Visit our websites:
www.titanbooks.com
www.mycityscreams.com

Did you enjoy this book? We love to hear from our readers.
Please e-mail us at: readerfeedback titanemail.com or
write to Reader Feedback at the above address.

To receive advance information, news, competitions, and
exclusive Titan offers online, please register as a member by
clicking the "sign up" button on our website:
www.titanbooks.com

A CIP catalogue record for this title is available from the
British Library.

Printed in the USA.

THE SPIRIT

THE MOVIE VISUAL COMPANION

MARK COTTA VAZ

INTRODUCTION BY FRANK MILLER

TITAN BOOKS

R... PH...
SUNDAY, OCTOBER 13, 1940

THE SPIRIT! WHO IS HE?

Daily Press launches campaign to discover identity of mysterious crim... **"Are you society's friend or foe?" asks editor Robert E. Gr...** fighter.

Ever since his mysterious in the capture of Dr. escaped mad-killer, known only secretly

On one hand he is obviously aiding society, yet on the other this mystery man is accused of causing the death of Eldas Thayer, a respected citizen, and is branded an outlaw the Police. ... the explanation? ...

His description, offered persons who have seen hi... Over six feet tall, wears mask and blue suit. Any... mation leading to the of The Spirit will b... ciated and kept co... All correspondence addressed to the ed...

...IC LEAD

BY Will Eisner

To the north of Central City, on a
hill overlooking the bustling metropolis,
lies abandoned Wildwood Cemetery.
Here, hidden in the tangled weedy growth,
is the hideaway of the Spirit. Accepted
by the police as a friendly 'outlaw' and
feared by the underworld, his true
identity is still a mystery.
Who is really the man behind the mask?
Every so often,
someone tries to find out...

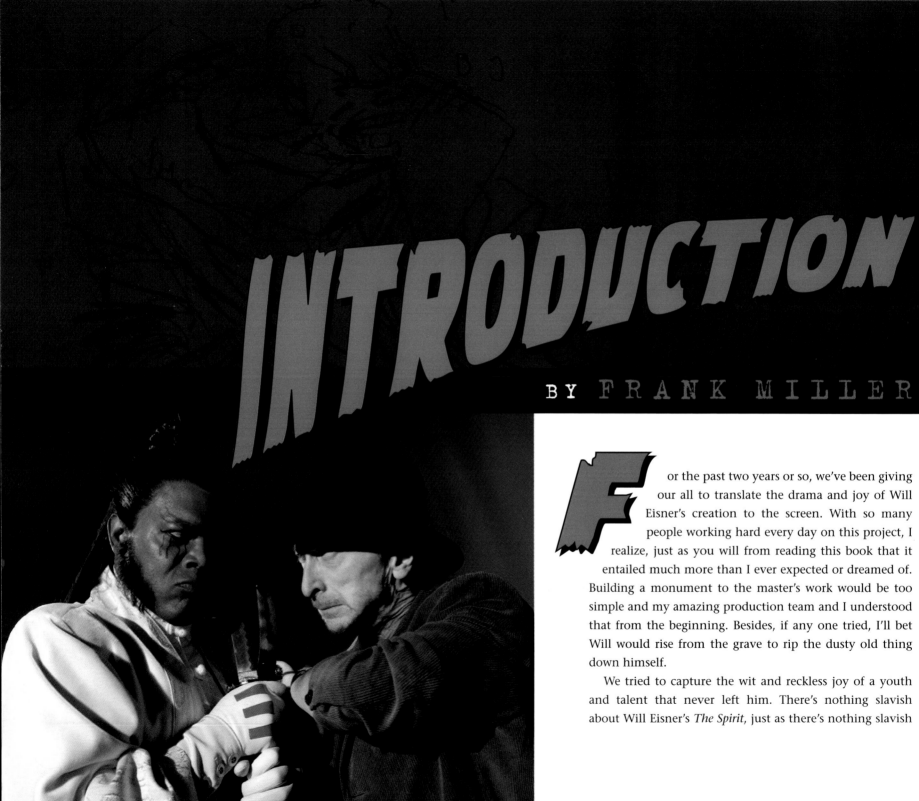

INTRODUCTION

BY FRANK MILLER

For the past two years or so, we've been giving our all to translate the drama and joy of Will Eisner's creation to the screen. With so many people working hard every day on this project, I realize, just as you will from reading this book that it entailed much more than I ever expected or dreamed of. Building a monument to the master's work would be too simple and my amazing production team and I understood that from the beginning. Besides, if any one tried, I'll bet Will would rise from the grave to rip the dusty old thing down himself.

We tried to capture the wit and reckless joy of a youth and talent that never left him. There's nothing slavish about Will Eisner's *The Spirit*, just as there's nothing slavish about Will Eisner.

This movie is my very best effort to do my longtime mentor justice. All through the shoot I've done my best to keep Will Eisner, that fiery old Bronx Jew, from rising from his grave to bitch-slap my sorry Irish Catholic face for doing him wrong.

This meant creating, not a piece of reverential, self-important tedium, but an artwork as ambitious and vigorous as its source. Come hell or high water, this movie was going to take chances, and offer something new. Damn the torpedoes. If I was doing this, I was going for it.

Long before we started shooting, I talked my head off about this movie to anyone and everyone and expected Will Eisner to tell me to shut my yap, do my job and "NOT F**K THIS THING UP!"

As always, I yearned to argue with him. I knew the old man was watching from somewhere, and that he'd want to know what I was after with the whole thing.

"Content," I knew he'd say. "Content." For the millionth time he'd say it, "Content!"

Will had a thing about content and we'd argue for hours about it. Often the content we discussed was precisely the content of this movie. The subject was and is 'The Hero'.

"He is the hero; he is everything," wrote Raymond Chandler, the Poet Laureate of hard-boiled crime novelists. I've adopted that quote as my motto.

This story, like many stories, is a definition of a Hero. Without a carefully drawn and tested portrait of the Hero, the whole thing falls apart like a house of cards.

People do spend entire careers on a journey finding out what a Hero is. Talent as widespread as Bruce Willis and Richard Donner and Raymond Chandler and Mickey Spillane have explored the concept of a Hero again and again.

Joseph Campbell's work is often misunderstood as a final word, as a finished essay, and because of that his work is

Contents Page:
Opener for "Death of Autumn Mews" *Spirit* story, October 9, 1949.

Opposite: Director Frank Miller squares off with star Samuel Jackson, who plays the Spirit's arch-enemy, the Octopus.

Left: Will Eisner! Golden Age comics creator, entrepreneur, graphic novel pioneer, inspiration for the annual Eisner Awards honoring excellence in comics.

PERSONALLY, I THINK EISNER IS OBSESSED WITH RAIN!

taken as rule. Not as the beautiful explanation for what makes a Hero. It is easy to pick apart his work just as easy as it is to emulate it. But Campbell was on a journey, he was exploring and discovering the many stages and nature of what a Hero is. As did Chandler, as did Spillane, as do Bruce Willis and Richard Donner, still exploring and producing.

It is my lifelong journey too. I came to realize this because of Will Eisner.

Making a movie is not as dangerous as warfare but it sure as heck can feel that way. Probably the closest most of us get to physical danger (with the exception of stunt-work) may be the electrical cables that snake the floor of the set. Worst of

ACTION Mystery ADVENTURE

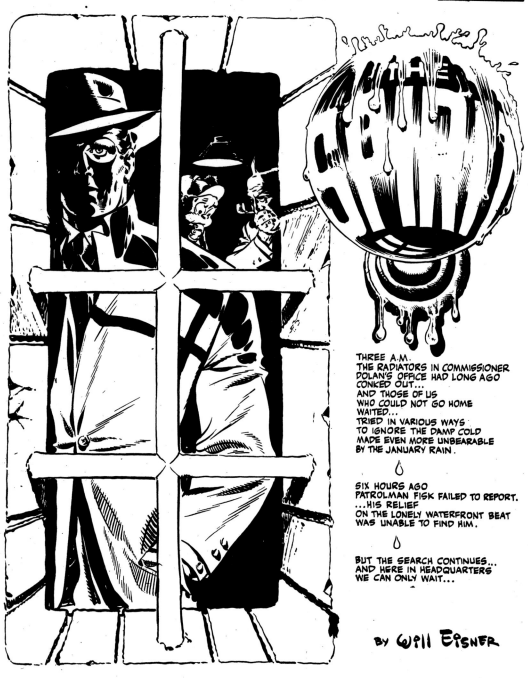

THREE A.M.
THE RADIATORS IN COMMISSIONER
DOLAN'S OFFICE HAD LONG AGO
CONKED OUT...
AND THOSE OF US
WHO COULD NOT GO HOME
WAITED...
TRIED IN VARIOUS WAYS
TO IGNORE THE DAMP COLD
MADE EVEN MORE UNBEARABLE
BY THE JANUARY RAIN.

SIX HOURS AGO
PATROLMAN FISK FAILED TO REPORT.
...HIS RELIEF
ON THE LONELY WATERFRONT BEAT
WAS UNABLE TO FIND HIM.

BUT THE SEARCH CONTINUES...
AND HERE IN HEADQUARTERS
WE CAN ONLY WAIT...

BY WILL EISNER

all, feet stumbling as they exit a movie-trailer down treacherous, class-action-suit-waiting-to-happen-fold-out steps that actresses miraculously maneuver in six-inch heels.

Nor are the stakes terribly high, in comparison to a war: a movie is, after all, just a movie. Hard-earned reputations and millions of dollars hang in the balance, but a movie will not overturn governments or annihilate a culture. And innocents are rarely killed, let alone slaughtered.

Making a movie is fun and thrilling and glamorous as all hell. It's also as hard a line of work as you can find. For everybody on the set, tenacity, resourcefulness, patience, and above all, your stamina and grace under pressure are tested and tested mercilessly.

Still, making a movie does resemble a military campaign. An awful lot of experts must converge to form a good crew. Logistics are a constant concern, so that actors have props and cameramen have lenses and, most critically, everybody has enough to eat. The hours are long and the players are unpredictable. Changes in strategy and tactics are both necessary and risky as hell. You spend long periods away from home and loved ones. You are distanced from normal, daily concerns and delights. You can forge relationships in weeks that are as intense as those that normally take years in that mist-shrouded, faraway place you call "real life". Most importantly, your hope of victory depends on clearly understood goals, dumb luck and maybe a dash of magic.

It's amazing how much a movie changes while you're making it. Sure, the script goes through many a permutation from draft to draft, as the writer develops his ideas, and, with mostly the producer's instincts and considerations, the script finds its voice and purpose before a single day of shooting. At least that's been my experience, as short as this experience may be. I work with an unusually strong and sturdy producer, Deborah Del Prete. She's a tough one: She's willing to work with me, for goodness' sake.

Once the movie is cast and the cameras are recording, it's

the director's job to keep the whole works on course. This routinely involves telling people things they may not want to hear, goading them, persuading them, all to keep the warship afloat and moving in the right direction, so you don't end up in an editing room full of delightful, crew- and cast-pleasing moments that amount to a pile of unseaworthy driftwood. We hear the sad result of that sort of disaster when a disheartened moviegoer mutters, "but the effects were great…" (OF COURSE the effects are great. Those guys are WIZARDS. But without all the other pieces in place, you're sunk. Nobody can polish a turd.)

The director's job is, first and foremost, to be the warship's captain: to remain ruthless in his destination, while ready for what shoals and unforeseen opportunities present themselves. But to never, not ever, let anything stand in the way of the warship's purpose.

The purpose of my solo-directing debut was straightforward: to adapt Will Eisner's masterpiece comic-book series, *The Spirit*, into a vigous and bracing movie. There was much to preserve and celebrate. There was also a fair amount to ignore or change.

The Spirit is, and will always be, Eisner's Spirit. Anybody watching me on the set could attest that I very frequently drew a storyboard for a given shot first as I saw it, then as Will might've seen it — and, in every case, went with what I saw as Will's version but it is not a rusty, dusty old monument to the work of my beloved Mentor, so much as it is an extension of what I know to have been Eisner's

Opposite: A noir-ish Eisner opener.

Left: Miller storyboard art, for an early scene in which the Spirit saves a woman from attackers.

Gabriel Macht as Will
Eisner's classic crimefighter
who rises from his own grave
to serve as protector of
Central City.

Right: Miller trying out guns
during pre-production.

Opposite: Miller storyboarded
the entire movie, such as
this early draft image of the
final confrontation between
the Spirit and the Octopus.

central intent: to create something new, witty, and exploratory. That's what he did. That's what I've done.

The Spirit movie's been one hell of an adventure, one that's made me love the world of comics more than ever. Eisner's soulful storylines and masterful cartoon art gave birth to the American Comic Book, sustaining its purpose and vitality for more than six decades.

And as for me, my producer, Deborah, and our hardworking crew; we all brought our best. Especially that old guy, who made the whole thing up.

Frank Miller
September 2008

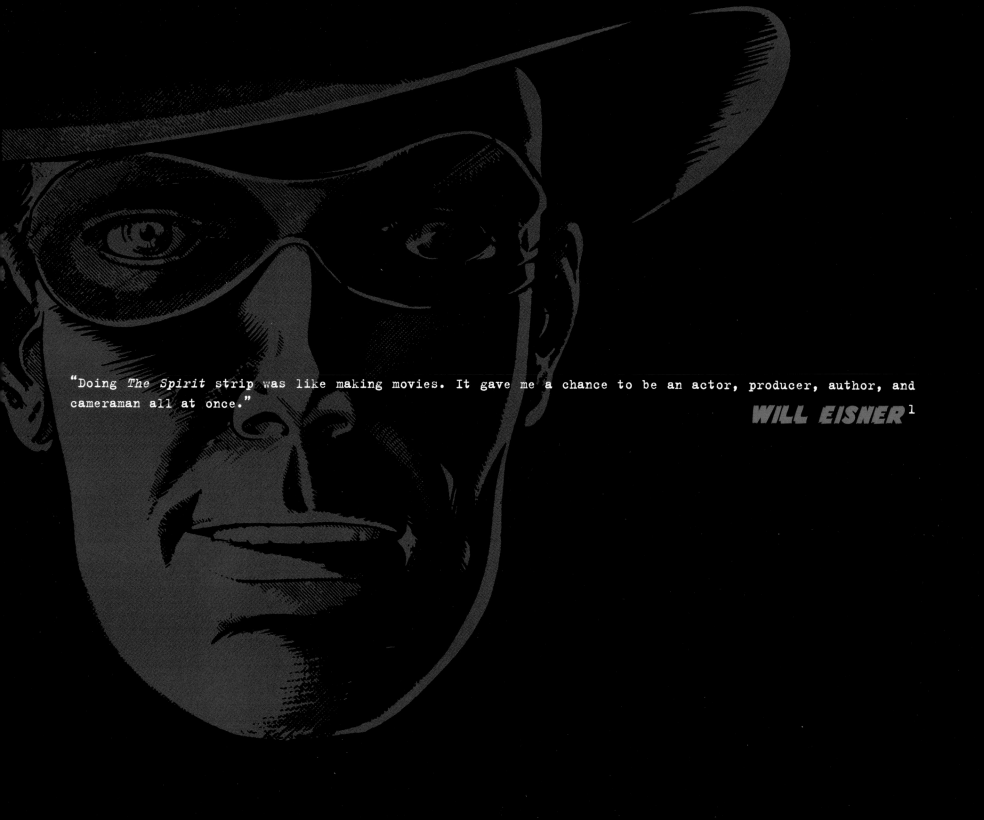

"Doing *The Spirit* strip was like making movies. It gave me a chance to be an actor, producer, author, and cameraman all at once."

WILL EISNER[1]

he tall man in the white suit, fedora, and dark glasses leans against the brick wall of the labyrinthine bazaar, watching a wizened soothsayer sit before a tray of sand, begging for baksheesh and prophesizing about Sheikh Ali Bey's daughter and the jewel of death set upon her forehead: *And she shall bring death to those who meet her until one of a hidden face shall come from the sky to stem her crimes and the time shall be of the quarter moon.* A pair of well-heeled Western tourists stroll by and scoff at such mystical nonsense, but the stranger knows a source of information when he sees one. He proffers a coin in a blue-gloved hand and asks the whereabouts in Damascus of a Dr. Gregg, a stocky man with a scar on his cheek. The old soothsayer reveals such a one drinks at the International Café. With a wave, the stranger strides off and the old man's bony hands trace an image in the sand. "Aye," he mutters, "he *is* here in Damascus and his face is covered with a mask... *today* will the prophesy come to pass!!"

The stranger enters the International Café, a dead-end dive where the flotsam of the world washes up. He moves past an undulating belly-dancer into a backroom where Dr. Gregg sits alone at a table, smoking and shuffling cards. The stranger knows all about him. Gregg was jeered as a quack in America, driven into exile by the citizens of Central City who didn't heed his warning about the disease that now has a thousand dying, a thousand lives Gregg's secret antidote could save. "*Now* they need me," Gregg grunts. "They're too late. I'm in exile! Say... *who are you?*" The stranger removes his dark glasses, revealing piercing eyes behind a blue domino mask: "I am the Spirit!" But the Spirit's plea doesn't sway the embittered doctor, who announces that today he has married Shellah, the belly-dancer, and reveals that her previous eight husbands all died on their wedding days. He chuckles that he hopes to beat the record, but what seals Gregg's doom, in the Spirit's eyes, is that the voluptuous temptress wears the jewel of death upon her forehead.

...MY CITY SCREAMS.

38

"In America I would laugh at that prophesy but somehow *here it seems real*," the Spirit exclaims as he escapes Shellah's thugs and reaches the doctor as a brick wall collapses on him. The Spirit pulls him from the rubble and Gregg, in a dying act of redemption, reveals where his notes for the antidote can be found. That night a shady gem dealer murders Shellah for the jewel of death, and is suddenly swallowed up in an earthquake. The Spirit, standing amongst an awestruck crowd, glances skyward — it's a quarter moon. In the brick-walled corridors of the bazaar, bony fingers pause at a drawing in the sand — the face of a masked man wearing a fedora — and drag across, erasing it. The soothsayer, sand streaming from his fist, mutters that the prophecy is fulfilled; a pair of tourists stroll past and scoff. And the man who came from the sky wings homeward with the antidote that will save the dying citizens of Central City…

Left: The movie emulated Will Eisner's aesthetic. This November 30, 1947 page inspired the "Eisner grate" set piece (see page 185 for the movie version).

Opposite: A young Eisner bones up on the Spirit's mightiest crimefighting weapon — the law!

The distinctive skylight of the Spirit's digs at Wildwood Cemetery, his hideout on the outskirts of Central City.

Opposite: Miller storyboard art of the Spirit in his hideout, with the skylight in evidence.

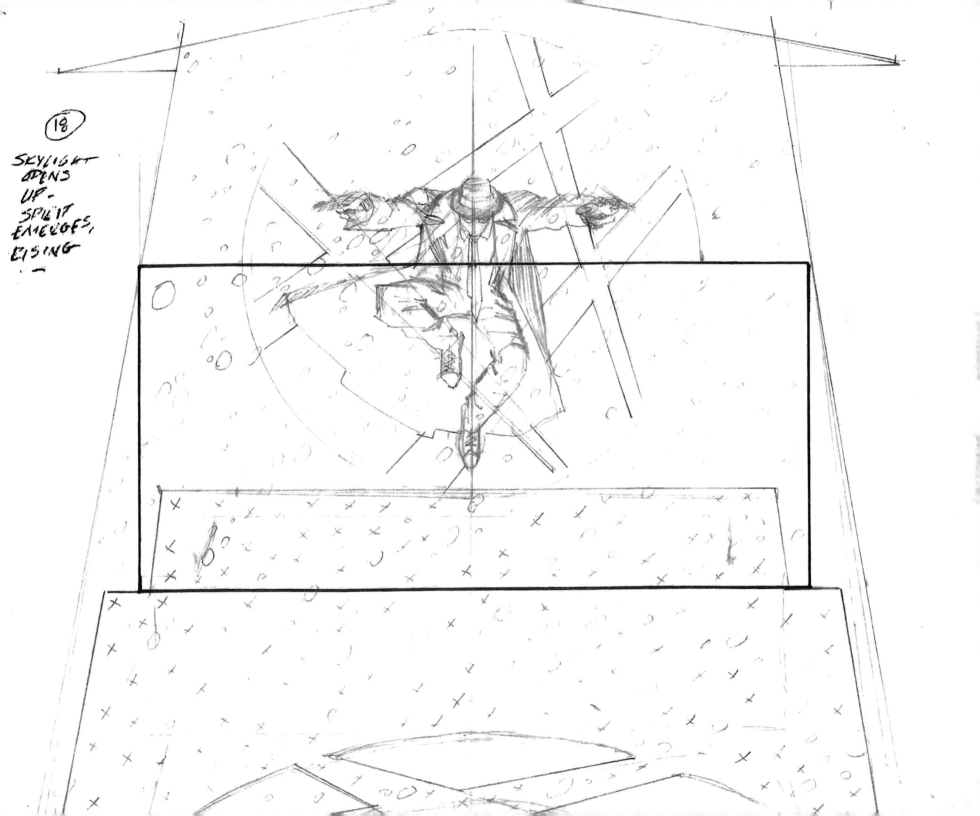

The above story, for many comics fans of a certain age, was their introduction to the Spirit. The tale, originally published in 1941, was among the full-color reprints in Jules Feiffer's book, *The Great Comic Book Heroes*, which was published in 1965. Back then, the Marvel Comics renaissance was in full swing, the *Batman* TV show a year away, and it was rare to see reprints from the legendary Golden Age of Comics, much less a hardcover collection with essays from a celebrated writer and cartoonist. *Heroes* was a book of genesis, a glorious archeological dig into a mythology born in the late thirties on the drawing boards of cramped studios around New York City. Here, in reprints of their seminal stories, was Superman, progenitor of the superheroes, leaping above the waters of a collapsing dam to rescue Lois Lane (he had not yet learned how to fly), while Batman seemed one step behind the Joker, whose nocturnal killing spree featured a deadly venom that left wicked grins on his victims' faces. The misanthropic Sub-Mariner emerged from his underwater kingdom to make mayhem in Manhattan, an anemic kid named Steve Rogers was injected with the super-serum that pumped him up into Captain America, and a deadly intrigue had the Amazonian Wonder Woman in danger from Mars, God of War and Axis agent (with a cameo by Italian Fascist leader Benito Mussolini). Joining this glittering pantheon, appearing like some profound statement as the final exhibit in the reprint section, was the Spirit.

Born at the end of the Great Depression and forged in the years when the world was at war, most of the hundreds of superheroes who suddenly appeared would soon vanish. A few seminal superstars endured, others vanished and were resurrected years later with revamped origin stories and costume makeovers, new heroes were born who reflected their times — like sentient organisms, superheroes evolved. But the Spirit was different. Like Athena, born full-grown in battle armor and springing from the head of Zeus, the protector of Central City burst upon the infant comics scene as a mature

and fully formed creation.

Jules Feiffer, who worked on *The Spirit* near the end of its run, wrote admiringly of the character's lower-middle-class background and ethnicity ("we all knew he was Jewish"). Like Batman, the Spirit didn't have super powers. But unlike Batman, who trained his body to "physical perfection" (as his origin notes), the scrappy Spirit got his workouts in the field, chasing down crooks and wading into them with legs kicking and gloved fists flying. "It took a mob to pin him down and no maniacal punch ever took him out of a fight," Feiffer wrote, pointedly distinguishing the Spirit's working-class crime-fighting (he had no big ticket items, like a Batplane) and slugging prowess (usually done with aplomb, tongue literally

planted in cheek) from the "rich idler's" school in which the likes of Bruce Wayne had to ritually don Bat garb and gadgets before he could jump in his Batmobile and go looking for trouble, where one of those maniacal punches *would* take him out of a fight.[2] To be fair, Feiffer was too kind — the Spirit could dish it out, but he took more than his fair share of lumps. Along with his wandering eye — where other heroes boasted pantheons of twisted villainy, the stable of *Spirit* characters included a bevy of beguiling females — the Spirit's resolve in the face of physical punishment was one of his charms.

Even at first glance, the Spirit stood apart. He eschewed the garish costumes and accessories that were *de rigueur* for the new breed of costumed crimefighter, favoring a blue suit and red tie, fedora, gloves, and blue domino eye mask (his white suit in Damascus doubtless a concession to the sweltering climate). Most of the early superhero stories made up in sheer energy what they lacked in plotting and artistry, but *Spirit* stories were always rich concoctions of adventure, mystery, romance, humor, and irony, with a sense of Fate brooding over the destiny of the characters. The artwork was cinematic (indeed, the Damascus story was steeped in the same exotic atmosphere that would be served up on the silver screen two years later in *Casablanca*), and extended even to the unique title design, always different in each story — the tale in Feiffer's collection pictured SPIRIT rising like the city gates of Damascus, the hero himself standing atop the towering letters with arms akimbo.

Will Eisner, the genius behind *The Spirit*, was born in New York City, the son of European Jewish immigrants. As a newsboy hawking papers on Wall Street, he immersed himself in comic strips, then the great daily visual entertainment. Will's father had been a backdrop painter for New York's thriving Yiddish theaters, but was otherwise poignantly remembered by Will as "a failed artist" who encouraged his son's natural love of drawing stories.[3]

Opposite and above right: Original Eisner art from 1947 and 1945 respectively.

Above left: The hero emerges...

In 1937, Eisner and Jerry Iger formed one of the first comics studios, supplying hungry publishers with product. Eisner was barely twenty, but his ambitions made him seem, even look, older, as writer David Hajdu describes: "Eisner was bigger than he seemed, thick all around and slumped from too many hours at the drawing table. His face was long and sober, though he could laugh heartily, if not easily, at himself. He wore gray Scotch-tweed suits and smoked a pipe, and he never brought up his unfinished education or his age."[4] Eisner and Iger rented a small space in a building near Grand Central Terminal that catered to bookies, and their staff of artists included future legends like Bob Kane and Jack Kirby. Eisner & Iger produced some notable creations, including *Blackhawk*, *Uncle Sam*, and *Sheena, Queen of the Jungle*, although the studio did pass on an adventure strip peddled by a couple of kids named Siegel and Shuster called *Superman*.

In 1939, Eisner sold his interest in the studio to Iger and left to create *The Spirit* as the lead feature of a full-color, sixteen-page comic book insert that Quality Comics publisher Everett "Busy" Arnold wanted to sell to the Sunday newspapers. It was a deal-breaker to have an artist own their work, but Eisner held out for a personal contract with Arnold that gave him complete rights to the Spirit, making him one of the first creators to broker such a deal in the hardscrabble, work-for-hire world of comics publishing.[5] The comic book section, its splash-page legend advertising "Action-Mystery-Adventure," debuted on June 2, 1940 with the first of Eisner's tight seven-page *Spirit* stories.

Spirit stories evoked Eisner's favorite writers, superb storytellers like O. Henry and Guy de Maupassant. The innovative cinematic style would later be likened to Orson Welles' *Citizen Kane*, but Eisner once explained the entire movie medium influenced him, even the experimental films of modernist and surrealist artist Man Ray. But a cinematic look seemed to come naturally to Eisner — years before a genre of moody movies earned the title of film *noir*, the Spirit's adventures were drenched in *noir*-ish darkness, shadows, and silhouettes. Along the way, as he helped invent a visual language for comics, Eisner discovered the secret synergy between the two visual mediums and applied principles of moving pictures to the static pictures on the comics page. "Eisner was the first to realize that the size of a panel equals, in filmic terms, the length of a shot in time," wrote celebrated magician, escape artist, publisher, and comics artist James Steranko. "Low-angle tilt shots deified the Spirit and surrounded him with a mysterious aura no other hero ever achieved. And at the moment of the highest dramatic intensity, Eisner would cut to a high-angle shadow shot that rocked you clear out of your seat. Eisner transformed comic pages into film storyboards."[6]

As Eisner revealed to interviewer John Benson, it gradually dawned on him that "films were nothing but frames on a piece of celluloid, which is really no different than frames on a piece of paper. Pretty soon, it became to me film on paper...."[7]

When he was drafted in 1942, and left his Spirit in the hands of other artists, Eisner's status as a professional cartoonist led him to Washington, D.C., where he was made editor of an ordnance journal and developed instructional comics for the Army. Eisner, always entranced by the artistic possibilities of the comic book, now saw its value as an instructional medium and after the war set up a company for that purpose. "In 1952 I became enmeshed in the wider use of comics," he later wrote. "My discovery, during the war years, of the potential of the comic strip as a tool for teaching and

Opposite and right: Consecutive panels from a 1947 strip highlighting Eisner's mastery of sound effects.

The main characters of Eisner's series, left to right: Ebony, the Spirit's sidekick; the Spirit; his love interest, Ellen Dolan; and her father, irascible Central City Police Commissioner Dolan. Ebony was one of the few "let's not" characters that didn't make the transition to the movie.

Opposite: The director contemplates the proper blade — where does he get all those wonderful toys?

training led to the formation of American Visual Corporation. This company, begun several years before, had grown so rapidly that the time available to me for working on *The Spirit* had shrunk to a dangerous low."[8]

Eisner brought *The Spirit* to a close in 1952, not long before an aroused public, educators, and opportunistic politicians branded comic books a peril to the nation's youth and enacted onerous censorship rules. "I had had it," Eisner once said of the atmosphere in which early comic book creators toiled. "It was very dispiriting. You were held in disdain if somebody knew what you did."[9]

Eisner, busy running American Visual Corporation, never returned to *Spirit* storytelling, leaving the hero and citizens of Central City behind as he headed off for new horizons. But *The Spirit* endured, kept alive for new generations of fans in reprints of the classic stories, from the tale included in *The Great Comic Book Heroes*, to reprint runs from Warren Publishing and Kitchen Sink Press, for which Eisner contributed occasional bits of business, mostly cover art.

The Spirit seemed a natural for the movies, but other than a disappointing made-for-television production (aired July 31, 1987), the character never got the big-screen treatment. That would change in Christmas of 2008 with Lionsgate's release of *The Spirit*, a live-action theatrical feature directed by Frank Miller, a fellow comics legend who once referred to Eisner as "dear friend and honored colleague… the Master."[10] Like Eisner, Miller brought a cinematic flavor to his comics art: "My interest in film has a lot to do with how I approach comic books," he said in a 1981 interview.[11] Miller, whose *Batman: The Dark Knight Returns* graphic novel electrified the comics world in 1986, had seen his subsequent *Sin City* and *300* graphic novels adapted to the screen in a style that redefined the term "comic book movie," and had served as co-director on *Sin City*. For *The Spirit*, Miller would not only make his solo directorial debut, but write the screenplay, storyboard the entire film, and be de facto production designer.

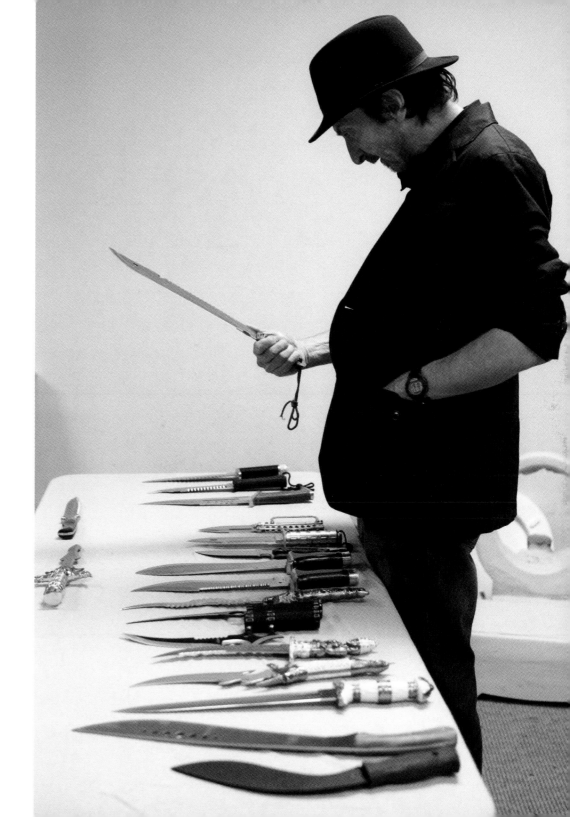

Handwritten notes on storyboard:
PULL IN FOR CLOSE-UP = NEVER PULL KNIFE S4 1 DAY FROM PRODUCTION AVENUE

Miller had agreed to direct in February of 2006, but the grand stage upon which his involvement was to be officially announced was planned for that epicenter of popular culture, Comic-Con International, the four-day summer convention that draws upwards of 100,000 fans to the waterfront San Diego Convention Center. The Con event guide listed the Saturday afternoon panel as including *Spirit* movie producers Michael Uslan and Deborah Del Prete, publisher Denis Kitchen, and "a major announcement," which was to be the Miller news. But the panel had drawn the biggest room in the place — Hall H, a 6,500-seat venue. Faced with possible embarrassment if the cavernous hall was partly filled, the production dropped the tease and Miller's directorial assignment was announced in the July 19 issue of *Variety*, a day before the convention. The *Spirit* team was still worried about the potential turnout — filming was more than a year away, and there wasn't even a frame to show.

"We were scared out of our minds!" co-producer F.J. DeSanto recalled. "I remember walking to the hall with Frank and he said, 'But we don't have anything to show!' And I said, 'We have you!' But we didn't know if we would fill that room — and we *filled* that room! It was amazing, watching everybody go crazy."

The creative journey lay ahead, but it had been an adventure just getting to the coming out party in San Diego. When Michael Uslan's Batfilm Productions optioned the property in 1994, prospects seemed bright. DeSanto had just joined Uslan's company and a theme running through his career for the next decade-plus would be the struggle to make the movie. "What happened after *The Spirit* was optioned is an odyssey, what I like to call 'Hollywood insanity,'" DeSanto said.

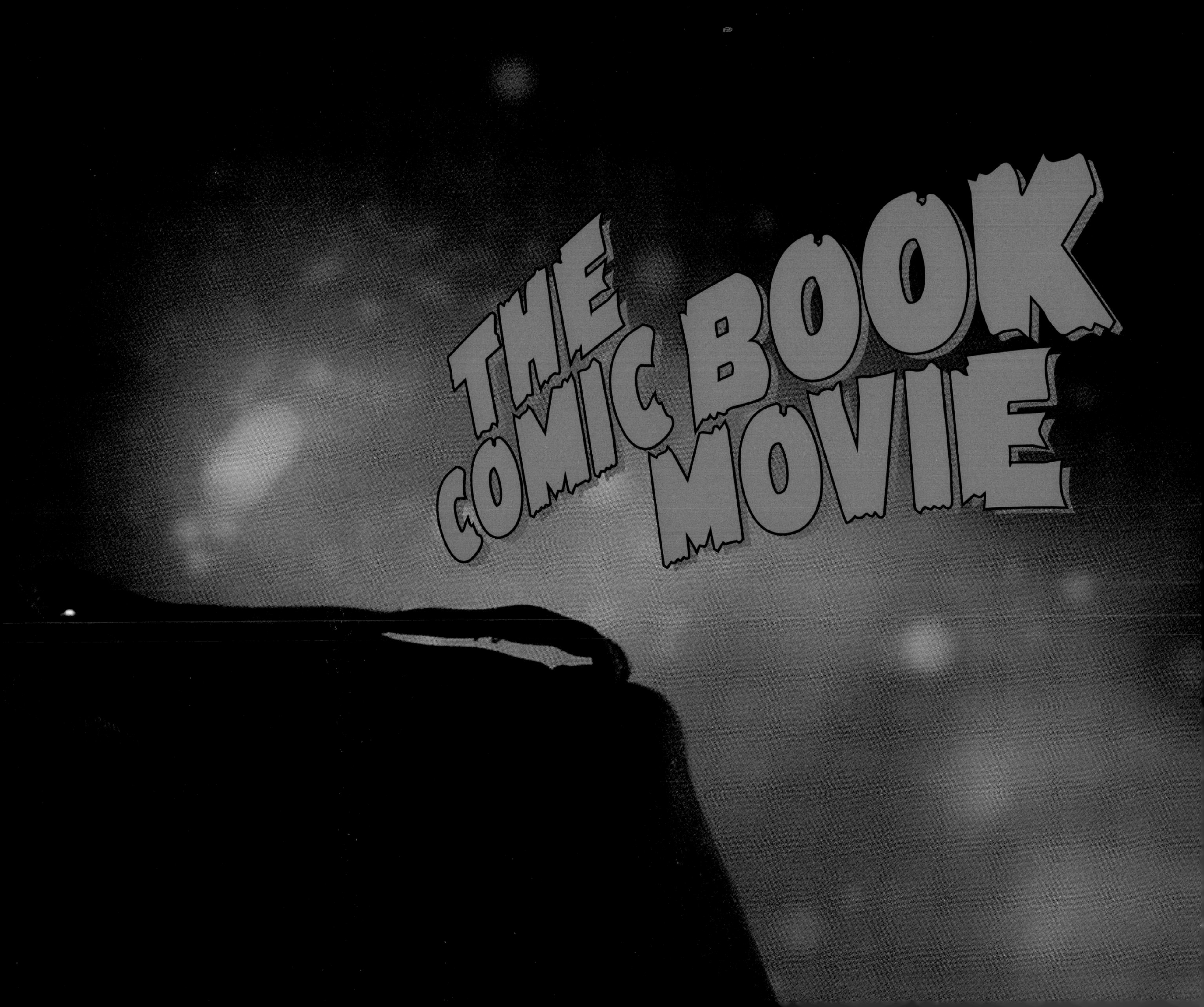
THE COMIC BOOK MOVIE

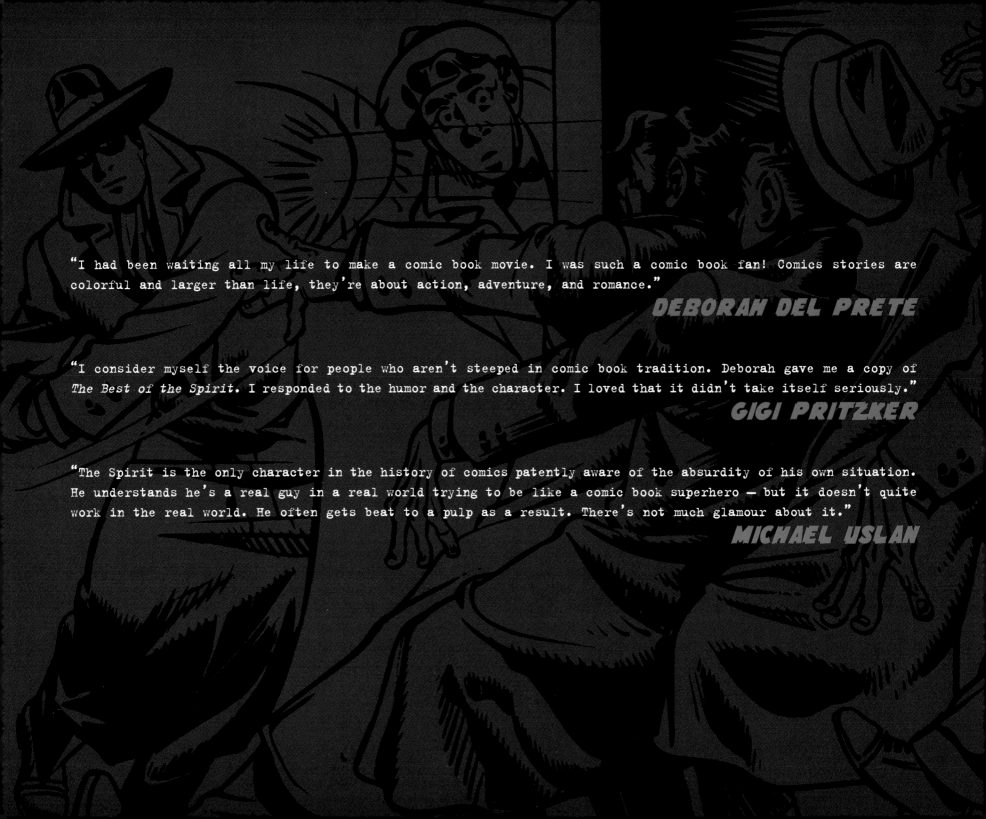

"I had been waiting all my life to make a comic book movie. I was such a comic book fan! Comics stories are colorful and larger than life, they're about action, adventure, and romance."

DEBORAH DEL PRETE

"I consider myself the voice for people who aren't steeped in comic book tradition. Deborah gave me a copy of *The Best of the Spirit*. I responded to the humor and the character. I loved that it didn't take itself seriously."

GIGI PRITZKER

"The Spirit is the only character in the history of comics patently aware of the absurdity of his own situation. He understands he's a real guy in a real world trying to be like a comic book superhero — but it doesn't quite work in the real world. He often gets beat to a pulp as a result. There's not much glamour about it."

MICHAEL USLAN

O ne day in 1958, a young girl named Deborah Del Prete was making one of her regular pilgrimages to the little comic book stand in the corner of her local grocery store in New Jersey. For a dime one could walk away with the latest adventure of Superman, Batman, or any of their costumed colleagues. But one comic seemed to jump off the rack: *Adventure* #247, a DC Comic, showing three young superheroes — Cosmic Boy, Lightning Boy, and Saturn Girl — judging Superboy as unworthy of membership in their superhero club. It was the first appearance of the Legion of Super-Heroes and Del Prete was hooked. One of the attractions was the sheer coolness of a girl superhero. When space and expense dictated she choose a special comic book, she decided to ally herself with that squad of teenage superheroes.

Overleaf: Director of photography Bill Pope lines up a shot while Sarah Paulson (Dr. Ellen Dolan) and Gabriel Macht take a break on the other side of the lens.

Left: Eisner art from *Spirit* story, November 3, 1946.

Opposite: Miller storyboard art, Spirit leaps with "And I am her Spirit" notation.

AND
I AM
HER
SPIRIT.

42

Many years later, Del Prete and Gigi Pritzker formed Dee Gee Productions, a New York-based company that produced corporate films, music videos, commercials, and documentaries. By 1993, the business partners made the move to Los Angeles to focus on independent feature film and theater work. Del Prete continued on a personal mission to collect all the Legion of Super-Heroes comics, both in *Adventure* and any other titles. She would become a Legion "completist," comics collecting parlance for a complete run of a character or title, including *Adventure* #247, that seminal

comic she'd read as a kid (and which cost considerably more than ten cents). Her quest was aided by annual visits to that comics Mecca, the San Diego Comic-Con.

"The Comic-Con then was about half the size it has become," Del Prete recalled of the early years when she had relocated to California. "Now it's so much about films and popular culture in general, but then it was much more comics oriented. You could go through the old books with dealers, and meet artists and writers. It was at Comic-Con, about fifteen years ago, that I first became aware of *The Spirit*. When

Original artwork (with whiteout!) of the seductive P'Gell, one of the leading femme fatales in Eisner's *Spirit* stories. In a 1977 limited edition *Spirit* portfolio, Eisner wrote: "P'Gell, the woman who was a totally amoral and often amorous adventuress, was perhaps his greatest nemesis." Notice the final color art in the photo, to Eisner's right.

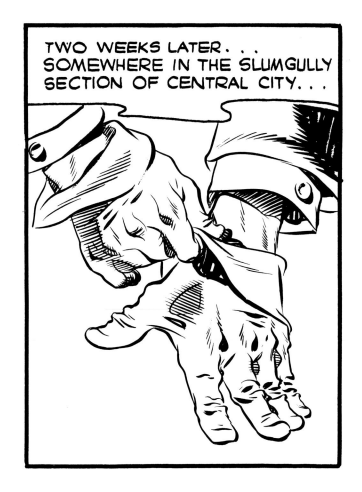

TWO WEEKS LATER. . .
SOMEWHERE IN THE SLUMGULLY
SECTION OF CENTRAL CITY. . .

you immerse yourself in the comic book universe you become aware of all the iconic figures."

In addition to her search for Legion back issues, Del Prete was on the lookout for a potential comic book movie property (Del Prete is "the comic book freak" in the partnership, according to Pritzker). Del Prete looked into making a Legion movie, and also made inquiries about the availability of Wonder Woman. However, the problem was the superstars of superherodom were tied up at major studios.

Del Prete didn't know it during her early years in L.A., but

one day the Spirit would come into her life, courtesy of producer Michael Uslan. Like Del Prete, Uslan had come into the film business as a hard-core comics fan, his passage into the comics universe coming at a time when comic books were considered kid's stuff and flew under the radar of the mass culture.

The Bowery of lower Manhattan has always typified skid row, a hard-luck district of bums and bars, flophouses and grindhouses. It was to this suspect part of town that two thirteen-year-old pals from New Jersey, Michael Uslan and Bob Klein, came in July of 1964, bound for what Uslan recalls as the world's first comic book convention. Uslan's nervous parents were escorting the boys and were aghast as they reached their destination — a fleabag hotel called the Broadway Central (years later the old place would collapse on itself). Inside, walls were crawling with roaches and they had to pass a seedy lobby bar, stepping over drunks to get to the elevator for the convention floor, a tribal gathering of two hundred true believers by Uslan's estimates. "At that convention, we realized there were other comics geeks like us — it was one of life's great revelations," Uslan smiled.

The two kids had become friends in the fifth grade when Uslan volunteered to share his locker with Klein, who was amazed to see a Superman pin-up decorating the inside of his new friend's locker. As kindred spirits, the two began exploring the great American mythology, even meeting many seminal creators. "It was an exciting time, we were learning about this Golden Age of Comics and that there was this whole generation and a half before us, and that Superman didn't always look the way he did, and that Batman didn't always have Robin," Uslan said. "It was fascinating and fueled our passion."

Along the way, the boys learned about creators virtually swindled out of their creations, about comics pros who were hard drinkers and lived harder lives, about lowly pay scales for a medium considered a notch above pornography. The

Right: Eisner art of Sand Saref, another leading femme fatale, who would go on to feature in the *Spirit* movie.

Opposite: Eisner cover art detail for first issue of Kitchen Sink Press's *Spirit* reprint run, 1983.

newspaper comic strips were where creators got rich and famous, their work followed daily by adoring millions — comic books were trash, even objects of fear and loathing. Uslan remembers watching Bob Klein's mother, fed up with her son's obsession, shoveling piles of his comics into a roaring fireplace — in slow-motion horror, Uslan watched the flames consume Spider-Man's debut in *Amazing Adult Fantasy* #15.[1]

In 1964, skid row seemed about right for a comics convention. To most fans gathered that summer day in the Broadway Central, it would have seemed a fantastical Buck Rogers's future to imagine comic books generating billions of dollars in motion picture box office.

In 1965, Uslan saw his first *Spirit* story in *The Great Comic Book Heroes*. "It was so different from the other stories, and what Feiffer wrote about the character made the Spirit sound like the greatest achievement in the history of comics — which it is! Bobby and I couldn't wait to get our hands on anything *Spirit*."

By 1979, Uslan was a lawyer in the legal department at United Artists (UA) studio and ready to make his move into the production end of the business with what he hoped would be the definitive *Batman* movie, presenting the character as originally created in 1939, that "creature of the night stalking criminals from the shadows." Uslan, in his twenties, knew he needed a heavy player to negotiate an option deal with DC Comics, who owned the character. A UA colleague named Charles Melniker offered to introduce Uslan to his dad, who had been a leading executive at Metro-Goldwyn-Mayer for nearly thirty years.

Melniker brought gravitas to Uslan's *Batman* dream and found a new career as Uslan's partner, pioneering the comic book movie. "I never thought at the time that comic books would be as dominant as they are today," Melniker recalled. "I remember meeting Michael in my office and he was so excited [about making a *Batman* movie], his sheer passion gave me the strong feeling it could be possible. When one goes in to

make a deal on a character like *Batman* you know you're in a big deal. The negotiation was very substantial and took a long time to negotiate — paying $50,000 in 1979 for an option was a very substantial deal."

Meanwhile, a year earlier Eisner had made a triumphant return to the greater comics world. Eisner always believed in the artistic potential of comic books, and had written and drawn what is considered the first graphic novel, *A Contract with God*, a slice of period New York life he called "eyewitness fiction." As *The New York Times* later observed: "In the 1970s, Eisner was reborn as a comic artist."[2] This renaissance would

set the stage for a chance meeting one day between Uslan and Del Prete.

Frank Miller credits Will Eisner and his *Spirit* as major influences, but pinpoints 1978 as the year Eisner assumed the throne as master of the comics medium. "Will had left *The Spirit* and then, very dramatically, returned like Richard the Lionhearted and stuck his sword in the ground with *A Contract with God*, which had a dramatic effect on my community of comic book artists. We all started looking at our work differently, as something that could exist not as an ephemeral series of pamphlets that disappear, but as a document that could last forever. It changed everything. Eisner wanted to see the medium explode and his return was as dramatic as when he showed up in the first place."

In 1993, as Uslan recalls, he and Eisner initiated discussions about making a movie. Eisner had relocated with his wife, Ann, to Florida and made special trips up to New York for meetings, accompanied by his entertainment attorney Susan Schaefer. *Spirit* discussions included creative issues of importance to Eisner. "I remember Michael was very concerned about whether *The Spirit* should be a period piece," F.J. DeSanto recalled. "Will said, 'Absolutely not! Whenever I worked on *The Spirit* it was always contemporary and reflected the day.'"

Melniker took the lead in negotiations and he and Eisner hit it off, often convivially speaking Yiddish together. Melniker had particular respect for Eisner's business acumen. "Very few people in the art world have much relation to what I call the real world, the material world," Melniker said, "but Eisner was very sharp on figures and would talk about a deal the way an agent or lawyer would talk about a deal! He was up to speed on everything. Eisner was very practical minded, and was very money oriented, and he wanted to give the least and get the most. At the same time, he was a very nice man and a very honorable man."

Melniker recalls *Spirit* negotiations as "tough," but a movie option deal was always complex. An option might include an up-front price or percentage, there were issues of an option's duration, merchandising, box-office calculations to make. There were also specific creative issues concerning the masked hero that Eisner wanted, and got, in the final option agreement — the Spirit couldn't be shown drunk, engaging in sex, or using a gun and "killing people mercilessly," Melniker added.

Eisner wanted *The Spirit* rights to revert back to him if Uslan's Batfilm company failed to get the movie made, but Melniker got Eisner to agree to a provision that allowed them to keep extending their option until they managed to put

together a movie deal. "We had a rather unusual thing in the area of extensions to the option, and I kind of patted myself on the back when it developed. I finally extracted a provision from Eisner and Susan Schaefer that after we exhausted our extensions we could forever extend that provision to prevent a reversion [of rights back to Eisner], if we paid $15,000 a year."

The deal was done — the pitching was about to begin.

In his teenage years as a camp counselor, Uslan discovered that after a day in the sun nothing quieted a gaggle of seven- and eight-year-old boys better than telling stories, and since the *Batman* TV show was then the rage, he made up Batman tales. It was a skill that would serve him well. "When I pitch, I don't see a room full of execs, I see my kids sitting around a campfire. It's my job to be the storyteller and hook them. This is your shot, it's showtime, you're on! And you either do it or you don't. I always started my *Spirit* pitches saying, 'What

Orson Welles and *Citizen Kane* are to cinema, Will Eisner and *The Spirit* are to comics.'"

But the "Hollywood insanity" F.J. DeSanto remembers was that no studio executive had heard of *The Spirit*. Moreover, they couldn't grasp the spirit, so to speak, of the character. The classic Hollywood dilemma is summed up in the *Sunset Boulevard* scene in which struggling screenwriter Joe Gillis is asked about his credits. "The last [screenplay] I wrote was about Oakies in the Dust Bowl," he replies. "You'd never know it, because when it reached the screen, the whole thing played on a torpedo boat."

Like the Dust Bowl drama that ended up beneath the sea, studio executives proposed bizarre *Spirit* makeovers. There was resistance to a comics hero in a suit and fedora, particularly when costumed crimefighters were ringing up billions in box office — put the Spirit in spandex, some argued. Others were stuck on the lack of super powers, and an alarmed Uslan listened as executives argued for making the character live up to his name and become an avenging ghost, cloaked like the Grim Reaper and armed with supernatural powers. "There are more people looking over their shoulder than looking forward," Uslan reflected. "They're afraid to do something a bit different. That was part of the struggle. But I promised Will that I wouldn't compromise, that we'd either do it the right way or not do it at all."

The concerns raised in those studio pitch meetings had been raised more than a half century before by publishers, when Eisner was developing his character. The irony was the stuff of a classic *Spirit* story, the case of The Reluctant Superhero.

When he left Iger, Eisner moved into another cramped studio in New York, this time in Tudor City, a development on a hill above Blood Alley, a stretch of slaughterhouses along the East River. It was here, in 1940, that the Spirit was born, where the final pieces of his creation fell into place one cold, rainy night. Eisner was burning the proverbial midnight oil on the first feature story for the comic book insert he was developing for publisher Everett Arnold, and had given his lead character, a tall detective named Denny Colt, the good looks and suave manner of Cary Grant — but with a twist. Eisner had read about a case where someone had gone into cardiac arrest, seemingly died, but come back to life. The idea of suspended animation fascinated him, and he decided to use it on his detective, who comes back as the Spirit, a "dead" crimefighter now free to operate outside the law. The Spirit's base of operations, his Batcave as it were, was a mausoleum in Wildwood Cemetery, the place Colt had been buried. But other than the twist of a man reborn, Eisner didn't want to make him a costumed or supernatural crimefighter. "In the wee hours of that night, I had roughed out the seven pages and I began writing dialogue," Eisner recalled.[3]

Suddenly, the telephone rang. Everett Arnold was on the line, arguing they needed a costumed hero to sell their feature to the papers. Eisner recalled that Arnold seemed to be on a saloon payphone — there was a slur to his words and jukebox music in the background. As they talked, Eisner drew a mask for his hero — like the Lone Ranger! — along with a hat in the style Arnold wore (reportedly, Arnold never got the in-joke).[4] Arnold argued the Spirit should have supernatural powers but, to their mutual credit, Eisner resisted and Arnold relented.

Eisner was always embarrassed by even the bare essentials of mask and gloves. In conversation with his friend Frank Miller, Eisner once deconstructed the superhero form: "The tights, the spandex, and the cape were straight out of the Barnum & Bailey Circus. Strongmen always wore capes, tight-fitting costumes. That was the symbolism. These were the iconographs that they [comic creators] chose… It's an absurd premise, anyway: a guy walking around in a mask and gloves, and nobody says anything. That's a reason I never liked superheroes."[5]

Despite what he felt were compromises, Eisner created a hero who broke all the genre rules and made up new ones, a

character who afforded all sorts of storylines and was presented in a unique cinematic style. It was this rich vision Uslan laid before Hollywood executives in his pitch sessions.

He went into pitch meetings armed with Eisner art to illustrate his points. Uslan declared *The Spirit* would not be a kiddy flick, and offered a splash page of the Spirit parting a curtain on a window view of Istanbul and the room of a voluptuous woman in red languidly stretched on a couch, cigarette smoldering between her pouty red lips, who announces, "I am P'Gell — and this is *not* a story for little boys!!"

Uslan served up Hitchcock-type tales thick with *noir*-ish atmosphere — Exhibit A was the splash page of the 'Lorelei Rox' story. Then there was "the whimsical Spirit" embodied in 'The Story of Gerhard Shnobble', a boy who realizes he can fly, but is punished by his parents and ordered never to fly again,

In his pitch meetings with studio executives, Uslan showcased Eisner's art as his best argument for a *Spirit* movie. This opener for the 'Lorelei' story illustrated the cinematic nature of the series.

an edict he obeys for thirty-five uneventful years. Finally, determined to show the world his amazing power, Shnobble leaps from the very rooftop upon which the Spirit is in a desperate fistfight with armed criminals. One crook fires at the Spirit, and a stray bullet kills the soaring Shnobble, who falls with no one having seen him fly.

Like in the classic *Spirit* tale 'Ten Minutes'[6] (another story retold by Uslan in pitch meetings), minutes, months, years were ticking away — no *Spirit* movie. Eisner, now in his mid-eighties, was restless. "He was impatient, really, all along," Melniker noted. "I remember distinctly we made the deal for the option in '94, we exercised it in '96, and he sent us an acknowledgment of the receipt of the option and said he'd like to be kept a little better informed and would it be asking too much to send him a quarterly or semi-annual report on the activities of what we were doing with the picture? Normally, if you take an option, you wait for something to happen. Eisner was one of the few who kept track of things.

"But there was something about *The Spirit* that everybody had a feeling that even though there was a lack of activity at a particular time, something was going to happen on this property, that it was going to develop into something important. So, maybe it was a good thing the people to whom it was pitched, who didn't have a vision for the property, didn't pick up the option. But that's what happens in this business. Some people have no conception of the depth of a project or a particular character.

In 2001, Deborah Del Prete and Gigi Pritzker had begun developing and producing feature films under the banner of Odd Lot Entertainment (a name with several meanings, including the stock buying theory that when everyone goes in one direction, one goes in the other, "odd" direction). They were also involved in theatrical productions and bought the Coronet Theatre on La Cienega Boulevard as home to both their film and stage enterprises. The Coronet was a venerable 265-seat house and under its proscenium arch had been stage plays from producer John Houseman's Pelican Productions, the world premiere of Bertolt Brecht's *Galileo Galilei*, and other notable productions.

A draw in owning the Coronet was it naturally attracted actors and writers. Del Prete and Pritzker had actor Dan Lauria as their artistic director, whose work included free Monday night plays that were a sensation among the community of film and TV actors and writers who welcomed a chance to work in the stage medium. Lauria was also good friends with Michael Uslan and one day, in 2001, Uslan dropped by to see one of the Coronet's Monday night plays and the actor introduced him to Del Prete and Pritzker. Del Prete was intrigued when she learned of Uslan's background in comic book properties. "I said to Michael, 'Look, I've always wanted to make a comic book movie,'" Del Prete recalled. "'We're independent filmmakers, we have our own money, we can do it ourselves. I've been looking for that kind of movie.'"

Uslan did not see the Odd Lot folks for a long time after that. When he was still frustrated in his *Spirit* quest, he went to meet with Del Prete in 2004. "We had a lovely conversation and then she said, 'You finally brought me something! What did you bring me?' I said, 'Deb, I'm bringing you the greatest creative work to ever come out of the comic book industry in the last seventy years.' She looked at me and said, 'Don't tell me you have the rights to *The Spirit*?' And I looked up into the sky and I said, 'Mama, I'm *home*!' She was the first person who knew about *The Spirit*! It was a magic moment."

The Spirit production team was with Will Eisner at the summer 2004 San Diego Comic-Con International. Odd Lot's Linda McDonough, a *Spirit* co-producer, recalls strolling the crowded convention floor with Del Prete and Eisner, whom she had met for the first time. "He was a lovely gentleman, charming. I think a lot of the character of the Spirit is actually Will Eisner's personality! I could just see him in his thirties, sweeping ladies off their feet."

Del Prete remembers Eisner marveling at the spectacle.

'Ten Minutes' is not only one of Uslan's favorite *Spirit* stories, but a favorite story, period. In the tale, the Spirit takes a backseat to Eisner's meditation on the vagaries of fate in the form of young Freddy, a loser going nowhere fast.

Below: Miller
storyboard art, a
knife-wielding
Octopus squares
off with the
Spirit. A major
sequence early in
the movie is the
hand-to-hand
battle between the
two enemies in the
muck of the
Central City
Mudflats.

"That was a great moment for me, and inspired me. I had waited my whole life to make *The Spirit* and I decided whatever I did was going to be for the good of the movie. That sounds so simple, but in the film business that's not the simplest thing. We were also putting our own money on the line with *The Spirit*. We didn't have the safety net of a studio, we couldn't afford to throw away millions on development."

In January of 2005, Will Eisner went into the hospital for heart surgery. Soon after, and suddenly, he died at age eighty-seven. Despite his advanced age, Eisner's passing was a shock to family, friends, and the entire comics world. "Will just seemed somehow… eternal," wrote Mark Evanier, Eisner's friend and comics historian.[7]

"Deborah observed that writers and directors were artists and they would be attracted to Will Eisner's seminal work of art," Linda McDonough recalls. Indeed, Del Prete was right.

Frank Miller had been on Odd Lot's A-list as a potential writer for a *Spirit* movie. Odd Lot would soon consider Miller as not just a screenwriter, but as a potential director. Miller had been a co-director with Robert Rodriguez on *Sin City*, but there were questions as to whether he could helm an entire production by himself. Del Prete spoke with Rodriguez and his wife, Elizabeth Avellan, and they had high praise for Miller as a director, particularly his ability to work with actors. After these conversations, Del Prete and Pritzker became determined to approach Miller for the job. Knowing Uslan would be attending the Eisner memorial in New York City along with Miller, they asked him to approach Frank and see if he would be interested in writing and directing.

At first, Miller demurred — how could he touch the work of the master, his friend and mentor? Miller walked away, but he soon called back with the words *The Spirit* production wanted to hear: "I can't let anyone else touch it."

Miller began work on the script over a six-month period in

2006, and by January of 2007 had a script Odd Lot was very excited about and wanted to make.

Looming over the production was the key issue of finding a distributor. Odd Lot originally envisioned a smaller-budget production, not a high-powered Hollywood spectacle. "We didn't want a movie that was overburdened by its budget, which frequently happens with studio-controlled projects," Del Prete explained. "Frank was very wary about dealing with the studios [after a bad experience in Hollywood]; for him that was incredibly traumatic. And Gigi and I were paying a considerable amount of money to Frank, and to Michael for the rights. There was a lot of risk."

There was also skepticism in Hollywood that the iconic comics creator could direct a feature. But then, Del Prete noted, they got lucky with the March of 2007 release of *300*, a huge box-office success. "Since *300* marketing was so much based on coming from the mind of Frank Miller, all of a sudden every studio was interested," Del Prete laughed. "But it was still important to get a studio that was willing to trust the vision of the director/writer."

Odd Lot Chief Operating Officer Bill Lischak initiated talks with Lionsgate Vice Chairman Michael Burns. Bill and Michael had known each other since the very early days of Lionsgate's formation. Together they created a deal which created a true partnership of funding, alignment of interest, shared worldwide performance and allocation of responsibility. The fruitful discussions, which were concluded on 15 May 2007, included studio production head Michael Paseornek. The Spirit would be the first of a three-picture deal between Odd Lot and Lionsgate. "Michael Paseornek is a real filmmaker and one of the best, if not the best, head of production in town," Del Prete said. "He made us feel protected and we knew they could be a home for this movie."

"'Studio' seems big and impersonal, but people sometimes forget all this stuff is about personal relations," Gigi Pritzker noted. "At the end of the day, a studio and production

company are collections of people who have to trust each other. Lionsgate is more like an indy [independent], a lean company without layers of people looking over their shoulders. They were thrilled to have capable partners, and they trusted us and left us alone to carry on the vision for this movie." The partnership, Pritzker explained, was a fifty/fifty split of production, marketing, and distribution costs. Odd Lot's half was a "patchwork" of equity financing with banks and international pre-sales. Odd Lot International made the bulk of foreign sales for *The Spirit* at the 2007 Cannes Film Festival.

The production also found a home for principal photography at Albuquerque Studios in New Mexico, a brand new facility that dangled the lure of tax incentives and rebates.

It was decided early on to follow a similiar production model to that of *Sin City*, which had been shot on digital high-definition with actors against greenscreen backings. Since editing and visual effects would be accomplished in the computer, *The Spirit* production saved the huge step of having to convert principal photography film to digital, only needing to output to celluloid for the final theatrical release prints.

Above: Director of photography Bill Pope and director Frank Miller. Pope (seen here in costume for his cameo in the film) was a superb choice to bring the director's vision to life, having filmed some of the most successful comic book movies of all time.

A key decision was to have a single visual effects house lead the effects work, a considerable challenge given virtually every frame of the greenscreen production was a potential visual effect. "We wanted a lead company and visual effects supervisor that was classy and had a reputation for delivering quality, cutting-edge work," said Linda McDonough, who negotiated the services contract with Albuquerque Studios and the visual effects contract. Although every visual effects house was eager to take a meeting with Frank Miller, Del Prete was worried *The Spirit* had budget constraints that might exclude high-end companies.

After a long search however, everyone's feelings were allayed. The Orphanage, a high-end effects house with offices in San Francisco and Los Angeles, was ultimately picked. Odd Lot was able to afford the Orphanage because of a unique partnership agreement that both companies embraced. "The Orphanage came through strongly in not just wanting to do visual effects, but to be involved in the whole process — they *got* it," Pritzker noted. "The Orphanage was there from pre-day one as part of the team."

A plus was that The Orphanage was up to speed on the production model, having been one of three main effects houses on *Sin City*, each of which had been assigned one of the hard-boiled stories from Miller's graphic novel series: 'The Hard Goodbye', 'The Big Fat Kill', and 'That Yellow Bastard'. The Orphanage had drawn the latter tale in which a cop, John Hartigan (played by Bruce Willis), takes on the city's power structure when he tries to end the reign of terror of a sexual predator, the title character who becomes a bloated, yellow-skinned freak after a series of medical operations. Their *Sin City* segment had been The Orphanage's biggest single job as a company, nearly 600 shots, with the challenge of turning the villain an ugly yellow and conjuring environments out of nothing. The work was supervised by Stu Maschwitz — a veteran of ILM's "Rebel Mac Unit," who supervised the space battle sequences on *The Phantom Menace* — who had co-

founded The Orphanage in 1999, where he operated out of the company's postproduction facility in San Francisco's historic Presidio.

For Maschwitz, who wrote the book on digital cinema (*The DV Rebel's Guide: An All-Digital Approach to Making Killer Action Movies*), *Sin City* was just the beginning. He wanted to take things to the mythical next level, and he would get his wish on *The Spirit*, becoming part of a creative partnership between the director, a core team of production principals, and every production department.

A key member of the team was director of photography Bill Pope, whose expertise in lensing comic book movies ranged from the comics-inspired *Darkman* and *The Matrix* to the

Opposite: Eisner panels from a 1950 story show the Spirit making his way from rooftop to rooftop in Central City — an image recreated in the film.

Above: Miller isn't afraid to let a black cat cross his path! Neither is the Spirit — cats freely roam his secret sanctum in Wildwood Cemetery.

second and third *Spider-Man* pictures. A comics fan as a kid, Pope returned to the medium as an adult when his son became interested in comics, about the time Frank Miller was coming into his own. Pope had even met Miller in the 1980s as a fan lining up for autographs at the Golden Apple comics store in Los Angeles. When Pope took his *Spirit* meeting with Miller, he brought in his first issue of *The Dark Knight Returns*. "It was the first pressing and was ratty and totally worn out, and Frank said, 'This is what a comic book should look like!' And he signed it.

"The thing about Eisner, I never liked him," Pope reflected of his boyhood encounters with *Spirit* reprints. "I was too young. The Spirit socks people in the jaw, that's his super power, and women fall for him, sort of a pre-James Bondian approach to superheroes. I liked the artwork. But Eisner was writing about grown-ups and a humor from the 1940s and '50s, an older humor, and I didn't get it — *Spider-Man* and *The Fantastic Four* spoke to me. But here's the thing — I signed on to do a Frank Miller movie. They had a production model in *Sin City*, they wanted greenscreen to create a stylized graphic look, and Stu and his crew at The Orphanage had worked out the data stream to work with digital capture. It was already set up when I got there — let's go!"

Other key production principals included art director Rosario Provenza, costume designer Michael Dennison, prop master Randy Eriksen, special effects coordinator Donald Frazee, set decorator Gabrielle Petrissans, makeup head Isabel Harkins, and stunt coordinator John Medlen. "My job was to protect Frank's vision and I made sure there were people around Frank who got his vision and could visually support him as a filmmaker," said Del Prete. "There's a magic moment when you have the director ready, the money is in place, and the cast is set. As a producer, it was my job to seize that moment."

"Deborah was like a locomotive," said Frank Miller. "The Production train had left the station and was speeding forward."

Opposite above &
below: Will Eis[ner]
brought sex to [the]
largely sterile
world of comics
crimefighters. [The]
Spirit's
"wandering eye,"
as Miller puts [it,]
was an essentia[l]
aspect of the
comics characte[r]
as adapted to t[he]
movie medium.

Left: Miller's
teaser poster f[or]
the movie, with
its Raymond
Chandler "mean
streets"
reference.

NEVER WORLD

"In his time, Will Eisner had the new story form of comic books, and the state of the art equipment he had were sheets of Bristol board and horsehair brushes and ink. In my time, the most exciting story form is the movies, and I've got Stu Maschwitz and the wizardry of The Orphanage, and Bill Pope and what he can do with a camera, and a cast that can bring life to Eisner's mythology.

"I decided that if I was going to do this job and do my mentor right, I would do so by respecting his intent, but not every last little widget of his work. I think if I had done something that was reverent, if I built a monument to *The Spirit*, a dear, detailed, absolutely faithful model, a certain number of fans would have loved me — and Eisner would have risen from his grave and ripped me limb from limb."

FRANK MILLER

he big lug in the black trench coat, Band-Aids riddling a face like a squared-off block of granite, lights up another cigarette and savors the one-two punch of a shot and a brew while Nancy, a leggy blonde poured into a fringed brassiere and tight black pants, shakes that bod on a stage behind the bar. Kadie's is a respectable dive in Sin City, and the pay-offs the proprietress makes to the right people guarantees it'll remain so. Sitting alone at a corner booth, trying out the new face a plastic surgeon gave him, is a killer on the run named Dwight who looks over at the big lug. "Most people think Marv is crazy," Dwight muses to himself. "He just had the rotten luck of being born in the wrong century. He'd be right at home on some ancient battlefield swinging an axe into somebody's face, or in a Roman arena

taking a sword to other gladiators like him."

As with Bruce Willis's Hartigan, Marv and Dwight, played by Mickey Rourke and Clive Owen respectively, were among the denizens of the *Sin City* movie, a breakthrough adaptation of comic books to the movie medium that began with *Sin City* director Robert Rodriguez, who defied the Directors Guild to have Frank Miller as co-director. Rodriguez, a master at creative and cost-effective visual effects (he served as his own visual effects supervisor on *Sin City*), had come off *Spy Kids*, and was planning a pitch to Miller about making a *Sin City* movie, when he had a revelation. "Instead of an adaptation of *Sin City*, we could just translate it, the way you drew it, right to the screen," Rodriguez explained to Miller in their shared *Sin City* DVD commentary.

YOU MUST **LIKE** GITTIN' HIT, SUCKER!!

Above: Miller storyboard art, Spirit fights with crowbar.

Left: Eisner *Spirit* art. The crimefighter may not use a gun, but he doesn't hesitate to use whatever may be at hand.

Next spread: The acerbic Dolan and his daughter Ellen, with the original comics inspiration below.

The key to the *noir*-ish, fever-dream *Sin City* comics imagery was filming actors on soundstages dressed with greenscreen backing — what Clive Owen described as "acting in a bubble of nothing" — and then, in post-production, filling in that void with stylized computer generated backgrounds and atmosphere directly inspired by Miller's artwork.[1] *Sin City* make-up effects supervisor Greg Nicotero singled out an Orphanage scene from the 'Yellow Bastard' story when he marveled at the final look to *Cinefex* magazine: "There is one shot that really exemplifies what was done with this movie. It is a shot of Bruce Willis running, then stopping and falling to his knees with chest pain. All that was there, initially, was Bruce Willis running on a treadmill on that greenscreen stage, then stopping and kneeling down. But in the finished shot, he is running through a forest at night, interacting with wind and trees and snow. It's an amazing shot, because none of that was real."[2]

The next Miller graphic novel to follow that greenscreen movie comic book model was *300*, a dramatization of the valiant stand Sparta's King Leonidas and his band of warriors made against invading Persian hordes at the pass of Thermopylae in 480 BC, which was published as a six-part series by Dark Horse in 1998. The film version, released in 2007, was a surprise box-office smash — a $70.9 million opening weekend — and had *Time* rhetorically asking: "Is it… the future of filmmaking?"[3]

But combining live-action with separately created imagery was as old as cinema. Traditionally, matte painting with brush and oils on glass or another flat surface often provided artificial environments that could be composited with actors filmed separately against a neutral backdrop. A 1923 *Motion Picture Classic* magazine feature on matte painter Ferdinand Earle noted with awe how Earle would "change the whole nature of screen productions… practically every set and scene in an entire picture can be the handiwork of a capable artist." In an early echo of Owen's "bubble of nothing," 1920s-era actors performed in front of black velvet, not knowing whether "they were acting in the palace of a Sultan, in a dingy hut, on a desert waste, or in a grove of cypresses."[4]

The arrival of computer graphics (CG) and digital image processing allowed filmmakers to produce and composite 3-D and 2-D imagery with a pixel-point control impossible in the photochemical era. Isolated effects shots gave way to all-greenscreen productions, such as *Sky Captain and the World of Tomorrow* (2004) and the *Star Wars* prequels. What set *Sin City* and *300* apart was not the technology, but the use of it. Just as Will Eisner once translated the visual dynamic of movies to the comics page — "film on paper," as he called it — filmmakers were translating the graphical quality of Miller's comics art to screen.

"The evolution of comic book movies, in general, has to be that audiences now accept more graphic approaches to things," Bill Pope mused. "Until now, [filmmakers] tried to make three-dimensional versions of comic books in a real place. You had comic book themes, plots, characters, angles, colors — but you didn't have the full graphic treatment. *The Matrix* was a pretty good leap forward, but the largest leap was *Sin City*, where it's clearly 2-D backgrounds with live people."

"In previous comic book movies you got the story, but a key part of comics is the work of artists, and that was missing," Del Prete added. "With *Sin City* and *300* you finally got the artist's work up there on the screen."

When Deborah Del Prete embarked on *The Spirit*, she barely knew Frank Miller — their joint appearance on the 2006 Comic-Con *Spirit* panel was only their second encounter. Del Prete laughs that the production became their "year of living together." At their first real meeting, she got down to business: "I said to Frank, 'Okay, you and I are going to make this movie and it's going to be us against the world. And no matter what, we're going to trust each other and make this movie right!'"

In his commentary for the *Sin City* DVD, Miller agreed with Del Prete's premise about the evolution in comic book movies: "With this magnificent greenscreen process this *is* drawing…."[5]

Frank Miller, who grew up in rural Vermont, recalls he was six years old when he approached his mother, held out a sheet of typing paper of his drawings that he'd folded and stapled, and announced *this* was what he was going to do with his life — make comic books. As a kid, he was inspired by the stoic heroism pictured in *The 300 Spartans*, the 1962 CinemaScope epic, and also absorbed the crime novels of Mickey Spillane and Raymond Chandler. All those influences molded a theme throughout his work to come — the lone, resolute hero armed with a code of honor in a corrupt world, the kind of figure of which Raymond Chandler once declared: "He is the hero; he is everything."[6]

In a classic scene out of the American Dream, Miller arrived in New York in the Bicentennial year of 1976, hard-boiled crime comics samples in hand. But he discovered superheroes "were the only game in town."[7] So he paid his dues, and began to push the limits. An early signature piece was 1983's *Ronin*, a six-part so-called "prestige format" DC Comics series about a masterless samurai who finds himself incarnated in a cyber-future world. In 1986, Miller made comics history with his *Dark Knight* interpretation of Batman.

Miller soon heard the siren song of Hollywood — and fell into what he called "a form of purgatory." He dropped out of comics for two years to write the *RoboCop* sequels, and came out mentally exhausted from the micromanaging, too many bosses and voices, the chaos of rewriting a script on set. Miller approached his drawing board after his two-year layoff

"terrified, just plain scared, feeling all on my own with no safety net." What emerged from that drawing board was the first *Sin City* story, published in 1992 by Dark Horse.[8]

In coming full-circle, the *Sin City* movie established Miller as a filmmaker. The personal challenge of directing *The Spirit* was to capture Will Eisner's vision, while imbuing the production with a contemporary sensibility. That approach evolved across six months of scriptwriting before casting began.

"I don't think anyone has ever done anything that was so much a tribute, yet uniquely its own thing," Del Prete noted. "Frank could look at the essential elements of [Eisner's] characters and take them into a contemporary world. We called the world the Spirit lives in the 'Never

World.' It's not any real time. The clothes and cars are all different periods, but there's also cell phones."

"With the *Dark Knight* I went for a Wagnerian punch," Miller reflected. "Leonidas was something ancient, Homeric. Marv goes back to Mickey Spillane. With Eisner's creation, I wanted to make him more resonant of the pulp era, of The Shadow and Zorro. We started with the things that had to be there. One is he certainly has a wandering eye, which is part of the debonair Zorro and Scarlet Pimpernel feel I wanted him to have. The Spirit's motives were always adult, frequently romantic, often plainly sexual. It was always about human stories in the midst of a romantic style and a time when Eisner produced stories of surprising naturalism. It was never about 'The Riddler's got the A-bomb and what do I do?!'"

There would be certain givens, including the addition of such classic *Spirit* characters as the irascible Central City Police Commissioner Dolan, who knows the Spirit's true identity, and Ellen Dolan, the commissioner's daughter and the Spirit's long-suffering love interest. But when analyzing Eisner's *Spirit* oeuvre for potential storylines and characters, certain things emerged as "let's not," according to Miller. A biggie was Ebony, the Spirit's African-American kid sidekick, despite the best of intentions a poster child for Political Incorrectness. Miller was also disappointed in the origin story and what Eisner could have done with a crimefighter who busts out of his own grave.

"Will was not big at finding fault with his own work," Miller smiled. "I thought the Spirit origin was a really crappy story and Ebony, who was probably created because of Robin and the popularity of teen sidekicks, was a bad idea. You can see where Eisner did some things grudgingly, some things badly, and some things brilliantly. He was at his best when he told a story about the lead character, or about the world and used the lead character as a vehicle to get you there. That's why I focused on the Sand Saref story as the basis for this

movie because I felt it was Eisner's strongest single story. It was so pure in its romance and wonderful in the way it presented the various virtues of the hero."

That story, published on January 8, 1950, had the Spirit walking the Mudflats of the Central City waterfront, parting the veil of memory to remember Sand Saref, the girl he loved when they were kids growing up in the slums of Central City's Lower East Side. Denny Colt was living with his uncle, a has-been boxer, and Sand's dad, a by-the-book cop, had taken it upon himself to watch out for the uncle. One tragic day,

Above: Miller creating blood-splattering effect for a ritual suicide scene.

Opposite: Miller storyboard art, Spirit up to his neck in the Mudflats. A copy of this image was blown up to decorate a wall of The Orphanage's Central City production "bunker."

Denny's uncle is involved in a petty crime, and when officer Saref appears, a wild gunshot kills him. Grief-stricken, the ex-boxer shoots himself. The dual tragedy drives Denny and Sand apart and onto separate paths — Denny to crimefighting, Sand to life as a jewel thief. (The Sand character influenced Miller when he worked on *Daredevil* for Marvel Comics, as he told *The Comics Journal* in 1981: "I wanted Daredevil to have a female antagonist, like Sand Saref in *The Spirit*. In fact, I ripped off the first Sand Saref story to do the first Elektra story… [but I also] put a harsher edge on the conflict."[9])

The young love story of Denny and Sand, told in flashback with actors Johnny Simmons and Seychelle Gabriel, formed "the heart of the movie," according to producer Del Prete. In the film, as in the original story, their paths dramatically cross in present time.

There were six major takes on the script, with changes that included having the Spirit, who would be played by Gabriel Macht, providing a narrative voiceover, instead of the Eisner-esque Central City washerwoman who appeared in an early draft. Along the way, producer Gigi Pritzker provided feedback. "I was constantly the voice of the ignorant person who didn't know comics," she laughed. "In earlier drafts there were leaps in story I didn't get, because I didn't know Sand Saref and all the characters. Deb and Frank would go back and essentially reorder things, make things more apparent. We wanted a movie that would appeal to *Spirit* fans, but also people who didn't know the character."

Many production principals noted that throughout the creative journey Miller seemed to be channeling the spirit of Will Eisner. When asked about Eisner's influence, Miller smiled and said, "The old man was around.

"There's a scene," Miller added, "where the Spirit is scurrying up one side of a rooftop water tower, he stumbles, and slides back down. That stumble, to me, was Eisner putting his foot in front of the Spirit's leg for a second and saying, 'You're still my guy.'"

But Miller also brought his own interpretation. For example, Miller dressed the Spirit in black, not Eisner's blue. (Though given that the limitations of old-style comics printing meant that anything black had to be printed blue, Miller reasoned that the Spirit in black had been Eisner's underlying intention all along.) Another fresh take was the development of the film's antagonist, the Octopus, Eisner's personification of a far-reaching underworld. Much like director Fritz Lang's criminal mastermind Dr. Mabuse, whose shadowy influence was felt but who was rarely seen in person, in the *Spirit* comics, the Octopus only appeared in glimpses, such as his striped gloved hands. "The Octopus was a cipher, but what I had on my hands was a movie," Miller noted. "The Octopus could not be played the way Eisner had done him."

Capturing the mood of Central City was another challenge. Other heroes guarded their turf out of duty, but Miller interpreted the Spirit's role in more romantic terms: "The city is treated like a woman because that's how the Spirit relates to everything. As he puts it, it's the love of his life."

Central City, Eisner's version of New York, evoked for Miller a specific section of Manhattan: "Central City exists between Jane and Houston Street." That includes the West Village, an historic district of narrow, winding, sometimes tree-shaded lanes bounded by old buildings of brick and brownstone opening into wide boulevards and taller structures with rooftop water towers. Across Jane Street one can look uptown and see the Empire State Building. "One of the things that bonded Will Eisner and me is a love of New York City, and a lot of this movie is a love letter to that," Miller explained. "The Central City the Spirit loves is one of tenements and water tanks — uptown to the Spirit is like Emerald City in the distance."

Above: Eisner art of Central City's skyline.

Opposite: Central City is faithfully recreated in the film as a town of bricks, brownstones, and water towers. The Iger Street sign pays homage to Eisner's first comics

This page and opposite: The Spirit, 2008, and The Spirit, 1949. The major sartorial change for the Spirit's movie incarnation was to dress him in black, not blue. As in the comics, the Spirit's distinctive tie is always fluttering in the air.

manipulation in the production's final stage.

"It wouldn't be accurate to say there was a plan in place before we actually executed it," co-producer McDonough chuckled. "It evolved, everything happened simultaneously. We actually didn't finish the visual effects contract on this film until we were done with principle photography, so it was a leap of faith for Odd Lot and The Orphanage to trust each other as we moved through production."

The Orphanage would be a full creative partner, assigning shots and supervising visual effects vendors, an unusual move in the digital age. "We didn't want to piecemeal shots out," said McDonough. "But in the last ten years, what everyone is comfortable doing is working with their own tried and true visual effects supervisor and portioning out work to different visual effects houses in a competitive environment where everything is up for bid. Deb had to defend this to the bond company and Lionsgate, which felt uncomfortable having one company in charge. If we'd gone to ILM, no one probably would have had a problem, but our budget would have increased by $20–$30 million."

"The bond company didn't want to have one visual effects company running the whole thing, but I *insisted*," Del Prete added. "I knew that with Stu and company I'd get an incredible dedication to the work. They were going to give more than if we just hired a visual effects supervisor to oversee various effects companies. There are other companies on this movie, but they're all under The Orphanage."

As the evolving production model fell into place, a "symbiosis," McDonough explained, emerged between Miller, Del Prete, Pope, and Maschwitz. "Everyone was so intimately involved in every aspect, from pre- to post-production. I think that was the only reason we were able to pull off this film on the schedule we had."

"Visual effects was not treated like post-production — it was treated as *production*," visual effects supervisor Maschwitz noted. "Visual effects wasn't an afterthought."

As part of Deborah Del Prete's production strategy, The Orphanage would not only supervise the work of other visual effects houses, but create the film's color scheme, a desaturated look with emphasis on specific colors in certain situations — red, in particular, would pop in the palette. In the process, principle photography and post-production essentially fused, with the work of many departments during filming having to anticipate the digital imagery and color

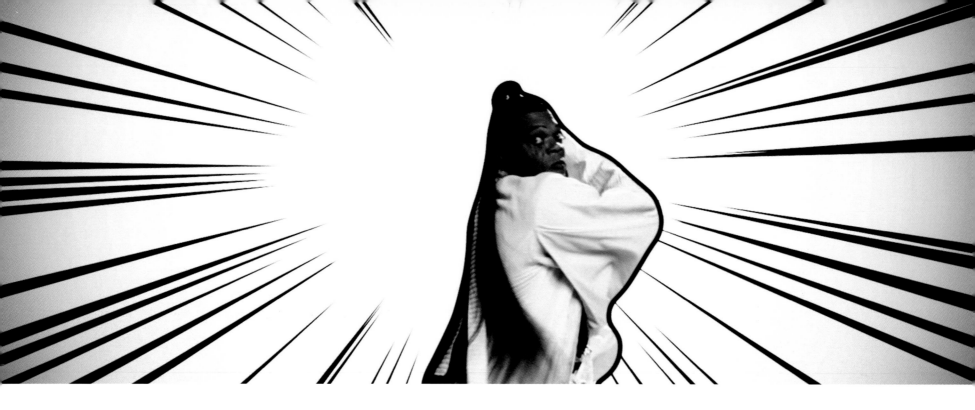

Previous page:
Greenscreen set up
for a scene in
which the Spirit
is caught by Hotel
Ares' decorative
ram's horns.

Above: A final
frame from the
movie, which
echoes, with its
use of bold color
and minimal
detail, the
"visual language"
Will Eisner forged
for the comics
medium.

Maschwitz detailed the challenge in a one-page 'The Spirit Visual Manifesto' disseminated among effects houses he supervised, which began: "This movie we're making here is unique. Yes, it's a 'comic book movie.' Yes, it's the third greenscreen movie with Frank Miller's name on it. But it is its own beast. We're gonna stand on the shoulders of *Sin City* and *300* and make The Next Thing."

Del Prete laughs that Stu Maschwitz was "Frank's love child," so closely in synch did they have to become to enable Stu to translate Frank's vision. "I had to become Frank, and he would be channeling Will Eisner," Maschwitz smiled.

Like many in the production, Maschwitz was already a Miller fan, but he had a lot to learn about Eisner and his *Spirit*. "I was certainly aware there was something called 'The Spirit,' but I didn't know how important it was. I think a lot of people are in my position. Eisner's character is probably the most

important and least understood moment in comic book history. Now that I've immersed myself in it, I love the quirkiness of the character. He is weird!

"When I first spoke to Frank about the project, what was interesting was he rattled off a list of the things he loved about Eisner's artwork, and it was like a list of things I love about Frank's artwork! In that moment, I realized how influential Eisner had been on Frank. I think of Frank as having a visual brevity, being able to communicate so much with very little detail and having a rawness and an emotional power that comes through in amazingly elegant, simple, bold compositions. I came to understand Eisner as a little more intellectual than emotional, a little more about detail than a lack of detail. Frank would say that Eisner had the ability to tell you everything you needed to know about, say, a detective, just by drawing one corner of the guy's desk, maybe showing an ashtray or a pipe. Little details, but they told you everything you needed to know about the guy's entire life. That was something I started to look for in Eisner's artwork, this kind of surgical application of just the right detail to give you a lifetime's supply of information about a scene or character."

Eisner's panels themselves are not crammed with detail, but draw the eye or emphasize action and spotlight characters with solid black backgrounds or splashes of color, swirls of shadow, perhaps a simple detail suggesting the surrounding environment. The production would essentially duplicate Eisner's technique, what Uslan calls the "visual language" he forged for the comics medium.

"There was a lot figured out in advance as far as the overall color scheme, a very contrasty film *noir* Frank Miller-type look, but we wanted to keep things minimal," added The Orphanage's Rich McBride, a visual effects supervisor who came onto the production as part of the previsualization ("previz") team. "A lot of times Eisner wouldn't fill in backgrounds, and we carried out that idea in the backgrounds for most of the sequences. Sometimes a background was solid colors, or what we called 'simple' matte paintings and set elements built digitally, mostly just finding the right detail to tell the story. This was far from how we'd normally see a digital background filled in with lots of [3-D] detail and having to fit in perfectly with the real world. This was a different way of thinking."

"What I was after in this movie was to incorporate that [philosophy] of using and presenting the right details to put you in the proper place and frame of mind, rather than burden you with too much evidence," Miller explained. "One thing that bothers me about our pop culture these days is that since we can now fill everything with detail, we tend to do so! There's never one spaceship in a movie, there's a hundred. And I've seen this happen in comic books. It just goes against my grain. I'm a real minimalist. I want to use this unbelievable technology to get three things right, rather than pack in a hundred things."

That visual minimalism was at the service of a photographic-based art design, as 'The Spirit Visual Manifesto' declared:

THE SPIRIT IS PHOTOGRAPHED

Sin City was a comic book brought to life. *300* was a moving oil painting. *The Spirit* is a movie. It was shot with cameras and lit with lights. This applies as much to the CG as it does the live action. There is no stylistic difference between the scenes with visual effects and the few scenes with none. We can be as stylized as we want as long as the images we make *could* have been made with a camera. We use photographic elements to create bold, graphical images.

"*The Spirit* is fundamentally photographed with a camera and owes as much to film *noir* as a comic book," Maschwitz added. "What that meant was the gauntlet was thrown down for me and my various crews to derive these comic book affectations in ways that could have been done photographically. This wasn't the one-size-fits-all greenscreen movie thinking some people have; that you light everything in a generic way and slap it all together later. This movie was very artfully and thoughtfully lensed by Bill Pope and his crew. Bill has been responsible for putting some of the most seminal comic book-inspired movies of our times on the screen. He's an artist and could take the intent and style of Frank's artwork and translate that into cinematography."

Principle photography would begin October of 2007, with the preceding months hectic ones of prepping for filming. "Deb allowed us enough time to figure things out, to have an efficient machine going, because when the clock starts ticking, and you're under pressure, time and expenses go quickly," Pritzker said. "Once Frank got on board, the time-frame condensed rapidly. It became a fast-moving train, but was still an amorphous thing. Once you start getting actors it becomes a real thing. They really got into the spirit of it, pardon the pun, and it took shape very quickly. The costumes are fantastic and were also a huge part of giving life to it."

Costume designer Michael Dennison, based in Taos, New Mexico, was assisted by Michael Crow and had a four-person crew in Los Angeles, with seven in a satellite work room at the Albuquerque Studios. Dennison remembers the mindset Miller impressed upon him at an early meeting. "Frank said to me, 'When you're designing the clothes, imagine you're drawing them in the panels of a comic strip and you've got to do that a hundred times a day! Pare it all down to the least amount of strokes, to what is the most important statement.' That was extraordinary. Think about what he has to do when he draws one of his graphic novels, and that's exactly how you take it. It's not about fluff, it's about getting the story said as quickly and succinctly as you possibly can. I loved the immediacy of that. That was the best thing he could have said to me."

Dennison, as with other departments, had to anticipate how The Orphanage, in concert with Miller and Del Prete, would orchestrate the movie's color scheme. "As opposed to doing an array of uber-colorful costumes that they would have to go back and desaturate, pull all of the color out, this was the reverse. My palette was very neutral, almost like I painted a picture in black and white with occasional pops of red or blue or yellow or silver. Anything I could do to capture the camera's attention, without blasting it with a

Opposite: Spirit costume design, front and rear views. Costume designer Michael Dennison notes the hero's trench coat was considered a "cape," one of many flowing garments worn by various characters.

Right and above: Exotic costume design for Sand Saref, with the final result adorning actress Eva Mendes.

PROJECTS

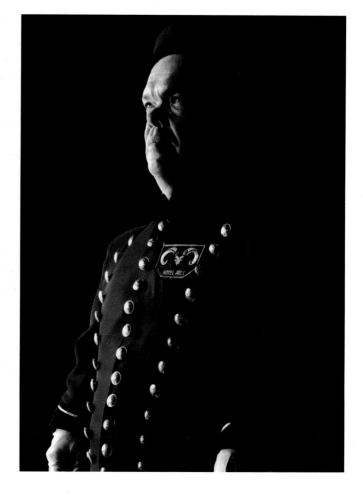

**Right and far
right:** Exotically
dressed Jewel of
India Hotel
doorman (Roman
Tissera; note the
Ashoka lion—
capital column,
India's national
emblem, on the
uniform's chest),
and Hotel Ares
bellhop (Hugh
Elliot).

field of color, made it better for later, so they could go in and computer generate the color any way they wanted. For example, for the Spirit I made an off-black trench coat with black top-stitching so they could capture the detail of the top-stitching and do whatever they wanted [with color] — take it out, make it white, red, whatever. Across the board, I gave [Miller and The Orphanage] the basic palette, pattern, design, and style of characters and costumes, a lot of stuff to key off. It's a whole new world now, with greenscreen — performers

are literally acting in space."

Santa Fe-based art director Rosario Provenza noted the set designs he worked up with assistant art director Todd Holland referenced *The Spirit* comics, with inspiration coming not only from Miller's screenplay but the director's own storyboards. "We didn't necessarily know what the backgrounds were going to be, we just knew it would have the flavor of an Eisner world, an urban, lived-in place. But movies are about that written thing on the page you have to bring to life.

Eva Mendes' Sand makes a cheeky photocopy, with her stylish costume's design to the right.

SUIT
COAT
& SKIRT

WAIST WELTING

LINING

SAND

BANK/LIMO

A gallery of Spirit costume designs. Front view of the dreamy Lorelei.

Front view of Silken Floss, Octopus's partner-in-crime, in Nazi dress.

CHINCHILLA FUR COLLAR

PARKA w/ SUBLIMATION PRINT & PUFF PAINT DETAIL

QUILTED

TUNIC

GLOVES

JODHPURS w/ BLK. SIDESTRIPE

Octopus costume designs. The Octopus's various costume changes reflect specific villainous archetypes. Overleaf: Details of his elaborate belts.

DUSTER

PIPING & EDGING

COLLAR

POCKETS

GLOVES

TUNIC & PANTS #1

PANTS #2

OCTOPUS

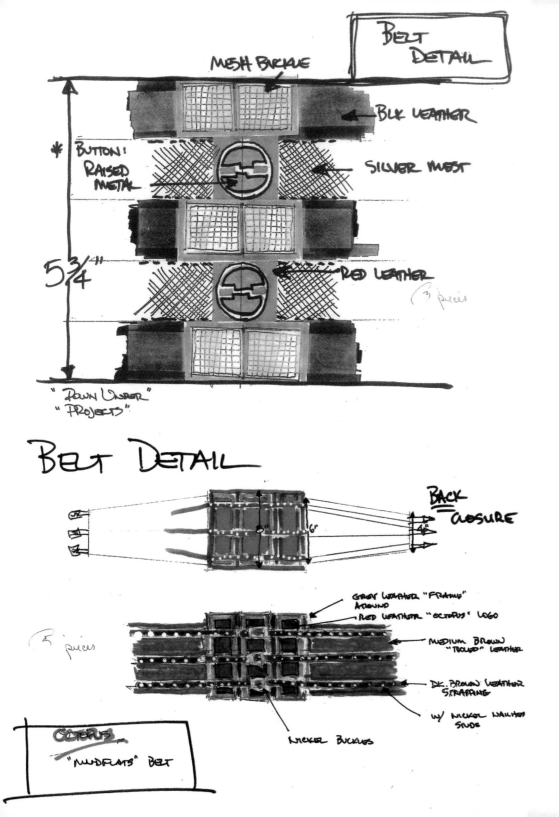

It goes back to the script, where the Spirit says the city is like a woman. She's a slightly battered but beautiful broad! Besides Frank's script, the visual guide was Will Eisner's comics and Frank's storyboards. And whatever Frank said or drew reinforced what his script was about. A lot of inspiration came from Frank's storyboards. I marveled at his drawings, they were so clear. When you looked at Frank's boards, you were in that world! Frank was not only writer and director, but basically production designer — it was all bundled into one, all your authority was there, you didn't need to talk to three other people."

Like the actors, prospective production department heads were auditioned. Set decorator Gabrielle Petrissans, who got the *Spirit* job, recalls flying to Los Angeles for her interview with Miller. In her experience, her portfolio usually got a cursory look during job interviews, so she was surprised by Miller's interest in her work. "Frank was also the production designer and he actually *looked* through my portfolio! He commented on some filigree work I had on a set, and a goat's head skull wired to a stave. I didn't have pretty living room interiors, so he liked the crazy stuff, I guess. But he talked the whole time about what he wanted. His assistant was laughing, my mouth was hanging out as I listened and I'm thinking, 'Oh, God, please let me work with this guy!' He's so *not* Hollywood. He doesn't have that ego thing. He's straight with you and generous with his vision. He wants you to see what he's seeing! The first thing he said to me was he didn't care about the time period — 'Just scare me.' That's a great thing for a set decorator to hear!"

Deborah Del Prete had known she had a great storyteller and visualist on the show — "This is Frank Miller, you think the composition of a shot is going to be off?" she laughed — but she was impressed by how quickly Miller took to directing actors.

Plaster of Paris, "the toast of Montmartre," first appeared in a
1948 *Spirit* story teasing a tied-up Spirit with her slashing
knives — as she would in the movie.

Above: Paz Vega embodies the knife-wielding seductress.

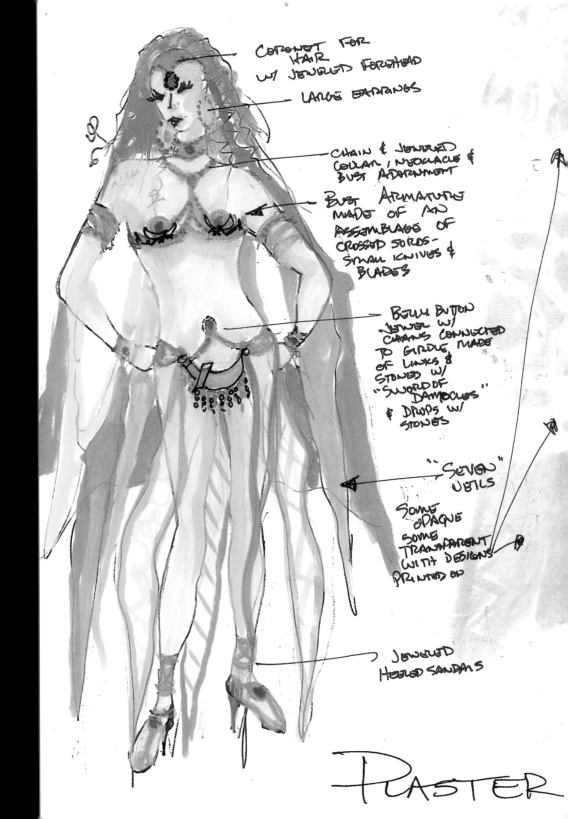

CORONET FOR
HAIR
W/ JEWELED FOREHEAD

LARGE EARRINGS

CHAIN & JEWELED
COLLAR, NECKLACE &
BUST ADORNMENT

BUST ARMATURE
MADE OF AN
ASSEMBLAGE OF
CROSSED SWORDS-
SMALL KNIVES &
BLADES

BELLY BUTTON
JEWEL W/
CHAINS CONNECTED
TO GIRDLE MADE
OF LINKS &
STONES W/
"SWORD OF
DAMOCLES"
& DROPS W/
STONES

"SEVEN"
VEILS

SOME
OPAQUE
SOME
TRANSPARENT
WITH DESIGNS
PRINTED ON

JEWELED
HEELED SANDALS

PLASTER

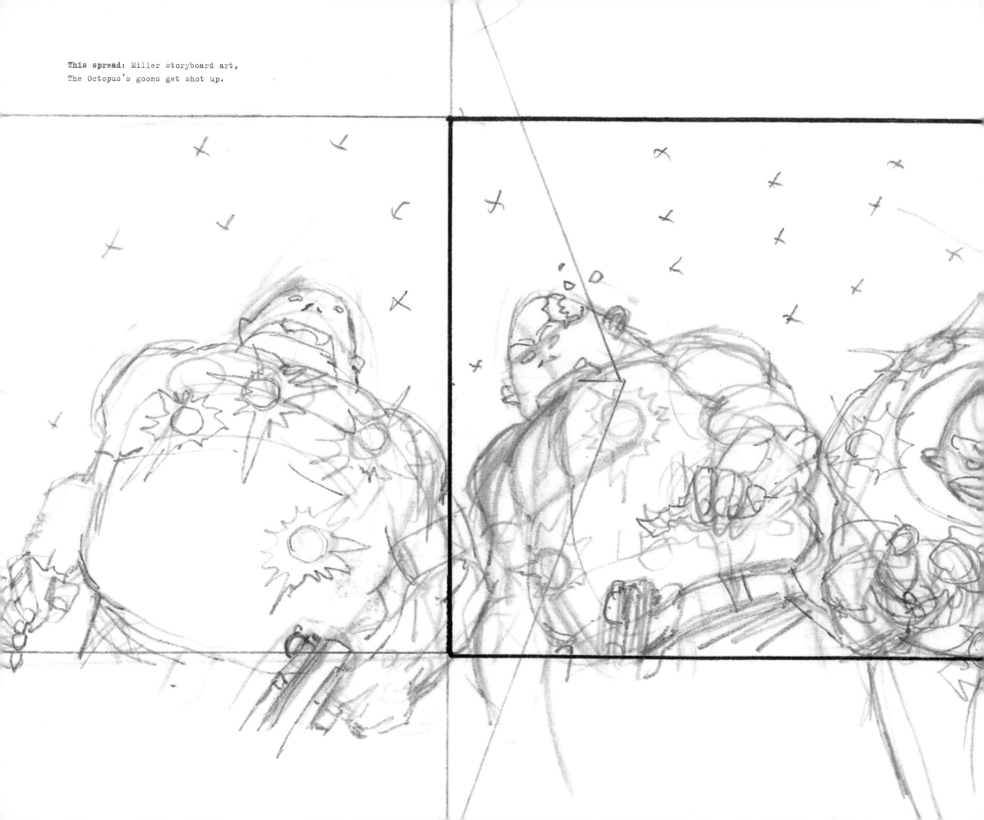

Above: Miller directs a scene on the greenscreen stage.

Right: *Spirit* production meeting, with, clockwise from the head of the table, Deborah Del Prete (producer), Benita Allen (1st AD), Frank Miller (director), Bill Pope (DP), Linda McDonough (co-producer), F.J. DeSanto (co-producer), Stu Maschwitz (VFX supervisor).

"Frank was a very quick learner," Del Prete noted. "He's a sponge person. When he was on the set with Robert [Rodriguez] on *Sin City* he sponged all that. He's one of the most observant people I've ever met, and you don't notice him noticing. Meanwhile, he's getting every detail of something in his amazing memory bank, he processes it, and uses it. In many ways, this movie is the story of Frank's journey as a director. He became a different person, he learned so quickly. By week two his ideas had become so much more sophisticated."

CAST OF CHARACTERS

"The Spirit is complicated. As Denny Colt, he came from the streets and was orphaned at a young age. He had a first love who left him and turned to a life of crime. But all he wanted to do in his life was to be a cop. Then, early on, Colt is shot in the back, and he never knows who his killers were. He's reborn, with an amazing physicality, through an experiment we learn about throughout the film.

"Whenever he's fighting crime, he's basically going after the guys who killed him. It develops the idea of, 'Who is this guy?' One of this film's major themes is man versus his own identity. In most superhero comics, the heroes know who they are, but nobody else does. In this, it's like everybody knows who the Spirit is, except the Spirit himself. I found that kind of funny."

GABRIEL MACHT [1]

This spread and following two spreads: The opening sequence. The Spirit is always ready to suit up and answer the call of his

Frank Miller's *Spirit* script opens with a cardiogram showing the flatline of a stopped heartbeat. A telephone begins beeping and the cardiogram spikes — the heart is beating. The Spirit awakes. Moonlight filters through the skylight of the mausoleum at Wildwood Cemetery as the lean, muscular, half-naked man walks across a floor full of roaming cats. He hears the distant howl of a police siren. On the phone is veteran Central City detective Sam Sussman, who tells him something BIG is going down at the Mudflats, out by the wreck of the old cargo ship — word on the street is the

The Spirit puts on his shirt and knots his bright red tie. He whips on a cape-like black trench coat, tugs on his black fedora, pulls on his black leather gloves. Finally, he puts on his black mask.

Outside, snow is falling on gravestones as the Spirit leaps over the wrought iron cemetery gate. Out in the streets, he climbs a telephone pole and jumps onto a power line and runs across it. He leaps through space and stands, poised on a rooftop, when he hears it — a woman's scream. He doesn't have time, but... he glares down. "My city screams. She needs me. I cannot deny her. I can never deny her. She is

ENTER
FRAME

CAT
ENTERS,
FOLLOWS
HIM

EXIT
FRAME

Del Prete and Miller reflected how "on the same page" they were, particularly in casting — when an actor auditioned, they instantly knew if that actor would be right. But one of their first decisions had been to not cast a big name actor as the Spirit, which proved one of the most nerve-wracking pre-production challenges both agreed during a joint interview. "At one point, we were scared we weren't going to find the Spirit!" Del Prete said. "The challenge was mostly about personality, because the character had to walk a fine line. You want him to be charming and loveable, but he's also a bit of a philanderer. He's also got to be the hero. The other problem was the oldest the Spirit could [look] was his early thirties. It wasn't easy to find an unknown with all those qualities. Frank was looking for a certain heroic quality, and he would read against these actors and challenge them, and they would just crumble, because there are few real macho actors today."

"But when you see them, they shine," Miller added, "and Gabriel really did."

Gabriel Macht, who had the requisite youth and square-jawed good looks, had done supporting roles and second leads in features, such as *The Good Shepherd*, *Black Hawk Down* and *Love Song for Bobby Long*, but was a relative unknown. When prepping for his star role, Miller insisted Macht not research the character in the color comics reprints, instead providing a thick book of black and white copies of original *Spirit* stories. The director also supplied his star with Raymond Chandler novels to further steep him in the pulp spirit. Macht also had to go through a physical transformation to get into character. He dyed his blond hair black, his brown eyes were fitted with blue contact lenses, and with a diet and exercise program he shed fifteen pounds. "Part of the genius of the wardrobe is they gave me fake shoulders which gave a real angular shape," Macht added. "A lot of what I was trying to do was pick out his physicality — the way the Spirit moves his head and shoulders, the way he looks at someone, the way he wears his hat."

Above: Miller storyboard art. Spirit puts on Fedora.

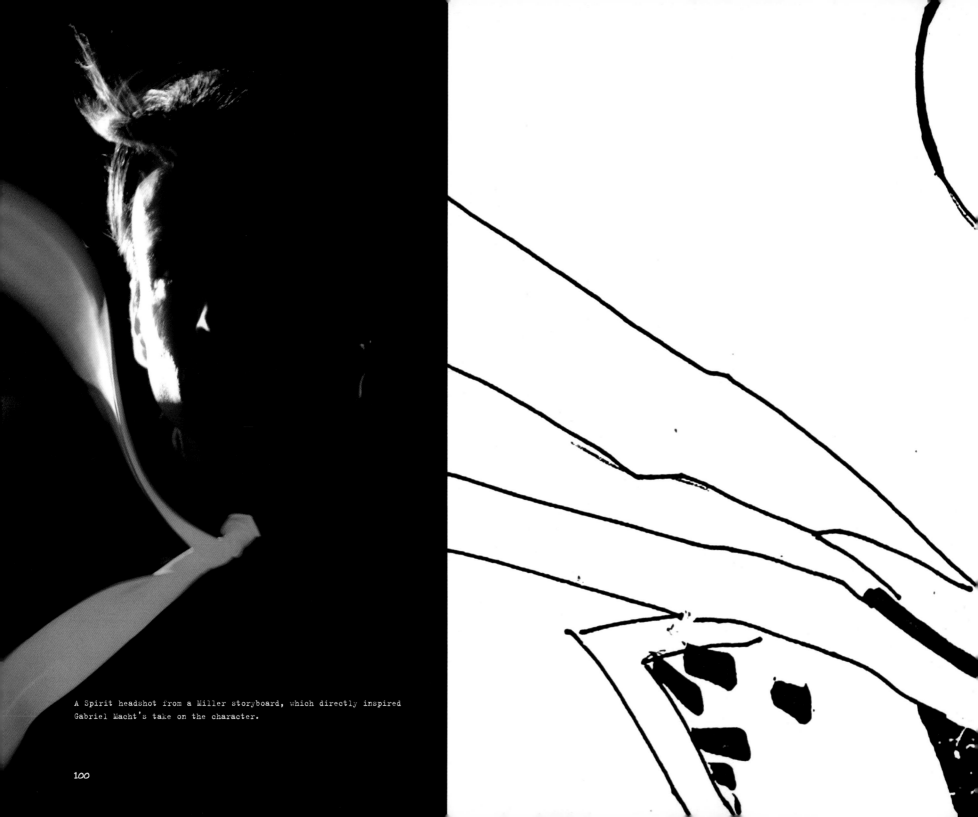

A Spirit headshot from a Miller storyboard, which directly inspired
Gabriel Macht's take on the character.

"There were so many permutations of what we had to have for the Spirit," costume designer Dennison said. "He had straight profile trench coats, running trench coats and flying trench coats [for wire work], trench coats cut in half, trench coats that were orange-lined to help The Orphanage key in their color. We called the Spirit's trench coat a 'cape' because its volume made it function like a cape, it's a very full body trench coat. But everyone had to have one piece of garment that flowed and floated so you got this wonderful, airy feeling."

Miller recalls Macht looked at one of his storyboards, a head shot of the Spirit, and said, "'The Spirit looks cool! Whenever I'm moving above the city, I want to look like that, I want to look cool.'"

"We actually re-shot a lot of his head shots to get just the right angle to make him look as good as he could," Miller noted. "The Spirit is very much his own character. He's very existential, a man who's been brought back from the grave, but he also has a wonderful sense of being sexy and debonair. And he found himself as I worked with Gabe. Between the two of us, I felt what emerged was a Spirit worthy of the source material."

The Octopus was essentially cast even before work on the script began, when co-producer Linda McDonough approached the director and producer about an established star she had in mind — Samuel Jackson, whose film work ranged from *Pulp Fiction* to the *Star Wars* prequels and the comic-book styled thriller *Unbreakable*. "Sam is also a great theater actor and I think people with theatrical training make better villains," she explained. "It may be because they have a melodramatic ability that film-only actors don't have, but Sam also had the subtleties to play against the theatrics, which would make the character multi-dimensional. I also thought it'd be fun to cast that role ethnically. Frank and Deb agreed to meet with him. Sam came to the meeting with his Frank Miller comic books, ready to have them signed — he showed up as a fan! They all fell in love, it was a great match. Frank finished the script with Sam Jackson in mind for the Octopus before we even had a deal."

The costume designer explained that the challenge was to bring the Octopus "out of the shadows." The Octopus emerged as the personification of evil. "We made it a morality story of good versus evil — and evil can take many guises," Dennison said. "The Spirit looks the same, basically a black silhouette with a red tie, his fedora, and quintessential mask.

Opposite: Gabriel Macht in wire rig set-up (note air blowers positioned in front).

Right: Samuel L. Jackson strikes a pose in an early Octopus screen test. His moustache and beard would be gone by the start of filming.

But since the Octopus is Mr. Evil, he morphed through different changes. When we first see him in the Mudflats, he's the first arch villain, which is the bad guy from Westerns, and he's in a bizarre version of a duster, with a hugely out of proportion cowboy hat. Later, he's dressed as a Nazi, which is good versus evil in war. I took all the high points of uber-evil and comic booked it up. It's black and white, good guys versus bad guys, which was wonderful, because that's how Frank illustrates — in stark contrasts."

"The Octopus is a psychotic, but also part of a genre you have to be true to," Jackson reflected. "Will Eisner had a great sense of humor, so there was an element of comedy to be maintained. Octopus is a bit theatrical, he puts on costumes, he changes. He refers to himself as a criminal mastermind, but he's also a scientist, a coroner, and runs a lucrative drug trade. So he has the money, the means, and he's crazy. A great hero needs a great nemesis — so the Spirit and Octopus were there for each other."

Dan Lauria, the "godfather of the movie," as Del Prete called him in honor of having introduced Odd Lot to Uslan's company, was cast as Commissioner Dolan. Since it was one of the most important casting choices for the film, they had originally kicked around a bunch of "name" actors for the role, but felt that the chemistry between the Spirit and Dolan was so important, as Dolan is a real father figure to Denny Colt, they wanted to be able to audition actors for the part. But after seeing many very good performers, they still hadn't found their man. Meanwhile, Lauria had been brought in to audition for the role of Sussman. Frank wasn't really familiar with him as an actor, but Del Prete had always harbored the hope he would like him enough to consider him for the Dolan part. She asked that Dan read Dolan instead of Sussman, "since there were more lines and Frank could get to see more of his ability."

"I had one reaction to Dan Lauria — no one else was gonna play Dolan. I went back and rewrote the Dolan part to remove

any nuance that would generate sympathy, to make him absolutely gruff from start to finish," Miller said. "You can not look at Dan without loving him, and I wanted him as caustic as Dirty Harry."

Ellen Dolan, a doctor who has to constantly mend the physical wounds the Spirit suffers throughout the story, was played by Sarah Paulson. Paulson, along with Lauria's Dolan, became what Miller called "anchor actors," counterpoints to the "unhinged" characters like Octopus and the Spirit himself. "When you got the gruffness of Dolan, that grounded you again," Miller added, "and all the insanity of this world had a context."

During casting auditions, Linda McDonough saw flashes of the Frank Miller that would shine during filming. If a casting director was reading opposite an actor and Miller felt he wasn't getting the desired performance, he simply got into the act. "Frank would just grab the script and jump in — he wanted to see the magic! That was his instinct, as opposed to someone who has gone through the machine of Hollywood. The school of thought is if an actor reading off a monotone casting director can't bring a performance to life, do you really want them? That can be valid, but I also think a lot of directors like to sit in that chair, like the Wizard of Oz, with a certain deference. But that culture of filmmaking is not Frank's background. What was organic and natural was to jump in and make the scene come to life! If he was auditioning actors for the Spirit, he'd read the Octopus part and did so with an almost child-like imagination. He was thrilled being part of making that scene, that moment, come to life — that kind of energy, when you're on set, is *infectious*."

The Chateau Marmont is a storied oasis on Sunset Boulevard in Hollywood. It was here that statuesque actress Eva Mendes came to take a *Spirit* meeting with the director, arriving as Miller was auditioning Scarlett Johansson. "I really loved *Sin City* and I was taken by *300* — I felt like, 'Oh this dude's got something going on,'" Mendes recalled. "I wanted to take a risk with Frank Miller directing his first solo film. When I got to the Chateau Marmont to meet him, Scarlett was still there with him. I sat down with them and it was one of those feelings — this really works. There was an ease to Frank, a feeling it was going to be good. When I was offered the part of Sand, I was like, 'Absolutely!'"

Like Mendes, Johansson knew of Miller and *Sin City*, but nothing of Eisner and his *Spirit*. But if Miller was directing something called *The Spirit*, she wanted in. "When she and Frank met, they mutually realized Scarlett's age was a little younger than the other women in the story," McDonough explained. "But just like Frank had fallen in love with Sam Jackson, he fell in love with Scarlett and decided to incorporate a character written for her."

For Johansson, Miller reached back into Eisner's treasure trove of female characters and came up with Dr. Silken Floss, who had appeared in a March 9, 1947 *Spirit* tale that opened with the beautiful and steely-nerved doctor saving a patient on the operating table. Floss next knocks the Spirit for a loop when she seemingly tricks him into a "marriage of convenience," and the story goes into high gear with a chase for the X-Germ, a Nazi-developed bacteriological agent in Dr. Floss's possession. In the movie, Floss would be an

assistant to the Octopus and have "more of a punk edge," McDonough noted.

Johansson was soon schooled in all things *Spirit*, and developed an appreciation for its creator. "Will Eisner was writing these great female characters at a time when people put women in a domesticated kind of box. Will's female characters were real femme fatales and looked amazing, with incredible clothes and beautiful hairstyles, very glamorous. And he gave them a lot of power over Spirit, because as much as they were fawning over Spirit, he couldn't resist those women. I think that's why those comics are so fun to read, there's a sexiness about that."

In addition to Mendes, Johansson, and Paulson, the women of *The Spirit* included Stana Katic as rookie cop Morgenstern, and Paz Vega and Jaime King (who played twin sisters Goldie and Wendy in *Sin City*) as two classic Eisner temptresses, Plaster of Paris and Lorelei respectively.

"What greater bodies to work with than the ladies I got to work with on this movie!" costume designer Dennison declared. "Once we were into the design and Frank saw the initial fitting photos, he'd make his comments. He might want to see more leg or décolletage or ask to split a dress so [an actress] could cross her legs in a scene. Once those corrections were made, we could just run with it. The great thing was everybody got into the fun of it, that they were doing bigger than life characters, and we could exaggerate parts of their body, highlighting different things. And, of course, the more we did the more Frank loved it."

The production emphasized "Never World" timelessness, but there were echoes of the source material's period. "This was a highly unusual movie," Bill Pope reflected. "It was basically the 1940s filtered through present day sensibilities and treated the way only one other movie [*Sin City*] has been treated. It was complicated, because actors were asked to act as though it were the 1940s, like they stepped out of a Mickey Spillane novel, but it was this timeless, stylized thing."

Make-up head Isabel Harkins noted Miller was looking for a glamorous, forties-era pinup girl look for *Spirit* women. "Frank loves his women, he likes them very sexy. I did a lot of jewels and feather lashes. I used crystals and pearls in the make-up to make Jaime King look like a mermaid, shiny and fish-scaly. For the eyes I used eyeliner, because Frank works a lot with the eyes, he loves the forties look of eyes looking up and having a mysterious, deep, piercing look. I gave softness to the lips, softness to the rest of the face, and worked with the colors that would work with the translation for the final product."

The Eisner influence put people in a period state of mind and Dan Lauria got Miller's permission to speak in fast and snappy period patter. "If you're a fan of 1940s film *noir* there was a rapid pace at which they spoke, unlike a lot of actors today who look like they're trying to remember their lines," Lauria said. "Speed was important in my character, it gave a real gruff edge. For Dolan I was really doing [the actor] Barton MacLane who, with Ward Bond, is one of the two cops on *The Maltese Falcon*. My character captures that forties element. That would be great, if my character reminded audiences of the old movies."

Eva Mendes also embraced the period flavor of her character. "I've gotten to live out certain fantasies on this movie, such as my love for the classic film *noir* of the forties, and my character is from that time. I knew nothing about Will Eisner before this project, but I've grown to love him. I love the way he drew my character specifically, and he wrote her perfectly, with so much pain and heartbreak, yet strength and an ability to overcome life's obstacles. Sand Saref is this

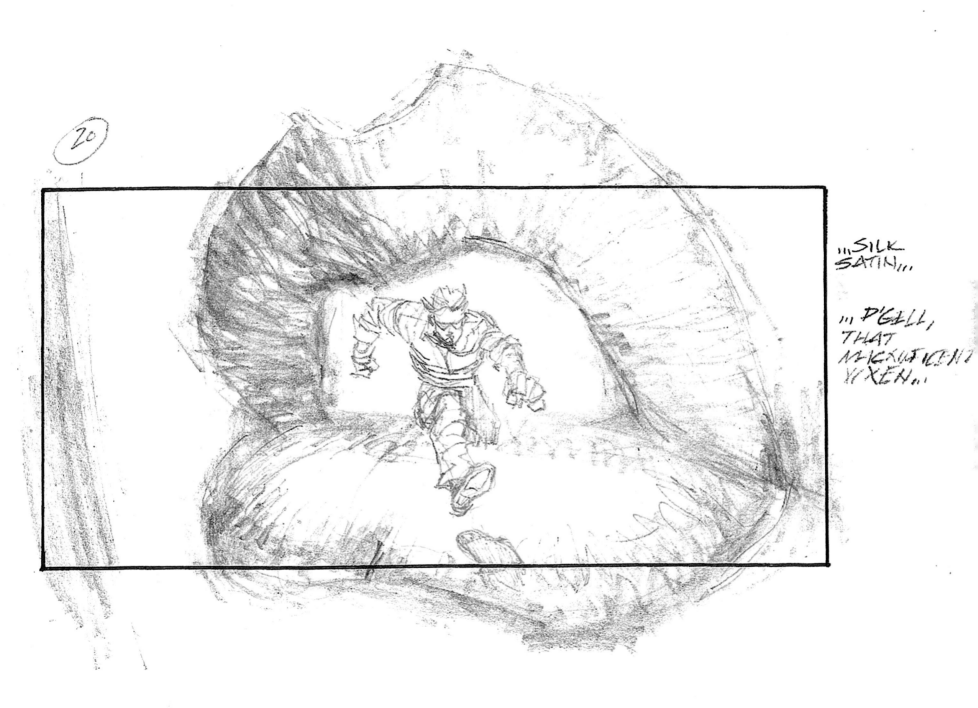

woman who's really a broken little girl. She grew up in the inner-city and her father was a cop who gets killed when she's thirteen or fourteen years old. She's brokenhearted and feels you can't count on anyone for love. The only thing you can count on is 'shiny things' as she calls them — diamonds. She's a jewel thief and diamonds symbolize something solid, something that won't go away. Her relationship with the young Denny was innocent and fun and crazy and emotional, and it's not that different when we see her and the Spirit together again, fifteen years later. There's still that fire between them, although it's not as innocent — they've both seen the ugliness of the world."

For the early Mudflats sequence, in which Sand and Octopus are diving and vying to find a mysterious sunken treasure, Dennison went for a sexy remake of the classic neoprene diving suit for Sand. "I found some phenomenal sparkle rubberized fabric that we recut and I built her boots into her diving suit; there's no line of demarcation between her boot and her leg and it goes up to a high seam in her hip. She just looks like a vixen. You either hate her or want to love her — which is exactly what everybody out there wants! They want that allure, to be invited into this whole scenario.

"And, of course," Dennison added, "Bill [Pope] brought his incredible eye to everything, and he'd get jazzed by a costume and run with it and make you look phenomenal, and that is the collaborative process. To put it another way, it was like Frank now had a lot of other hands doing parts of his [comics] panels for him, and all he had to do was direct it. His vision was coming to life in front of him."

Left: The fedora-wearing director poses with some of his actresses.

Opposite: The star-crossed sweethearts meet again.

Miller gave a lot of thought to casting even the minor roles and players. In some of the early script drafts, there were various henchmen, but they all felt somewhat generic. Eventually Frank came up with the concept of all of the Octopus's henchmen being clones, men produced by him and therefore very disposable. It made what was a group of small roles into a much bigger role for one actor. Frank wanted someone who would project a kind of slow-witted, benign evil — a look reflected in his drawings for the character: bald dome-topped, dome-shaped grinning idiots. "We kept getting close but not quite there, until Frank requested that the casting directors bring in Louis Lombardi, who he remembered from the series *24*," Del Prete said. "I couldn't

believe it when he walked in — he was Frank's drawings come to life. I guess somehow Frank had channeled him and once Louis read the lines for us, we were done casting that part. He was truly perfect."

Frank and Deborah originally had planned to cast Dan Lauria as Sussman, the veteran cop who calls the Spirit to the mudflats, an event that launches the Sand Saref story. After Frank decided Dan was the perfect Dolan they were left without a Sussman. By that time the filmmakers were already in Albuquerque, so they started looking at the local talent. Luckily for them the very experienced character actor Dan Gerrity had recently located to New Mexico and they were happy to get him.

Because Miller's vision is that of an artist, he had many strong physical images in mind for each role. Del Prete recalled, "It was very important to him that we start the film with a woman in distress being saved by the Spirit, to establish his heroism right up front. And for Frank, that image was a woman with large, terrified eyes staring up in the darkness. Kimberly Cox personified that, plus she had a great scream! For the sleazy and crooked antiques dealer, Donenfeld, we saw a lot of great character actors but when Richard Portnow came in, he captured just the right amount of indignant sophistication cloaking a debauched underbelly. For his mild-mannered assistant, Seth, Miller decided he didn't need to look very far. His own assistant, Mark Del Gallo, while not quite as mild-mannered, was a talented young actor and had just the look and style he wanted for the hapless Seth."

Miller and Del Prete enjoy inside jokes and there are a number of them throughout The Spirit. Many of them refer to the original Eisner stories, but when Frank wrote a small role for a wino who encounters the Spirit on the docks after the masked crusader has been stabbed with a machete by Plaster of Paris, they just couldn't resist giving the role to Del Prete's actor/writer husband, T. Jay O'Brien. The Wino's only line to the nearly unconscious, reeling Spirit is "I know the feeling. You should meet my wife!" But Del Prete considered the best inside joke of the film to be Miller playing the role of the ill fated, highly nervous Officer Liebowitz. "I particularly wanted Frank to play this role since the character was going to be decapitated and we were going to have to make a life cast of his head. Not only could I then at any time ask for the crew to 'bring me the head of Frank Miller,' but it would give me one of the greatest souvenirs of any film I've ever made. I keep it in my office on the second level of my glass coffee table and it's quite the conversation piece."

Above and right: "Bring me the head of Frank Miller." Miller in his role as Liebowitz, and the life cast of his head.

Below: Deborah Del Prete's husband T. Jay O'Brien, in his cameo as the Wino.

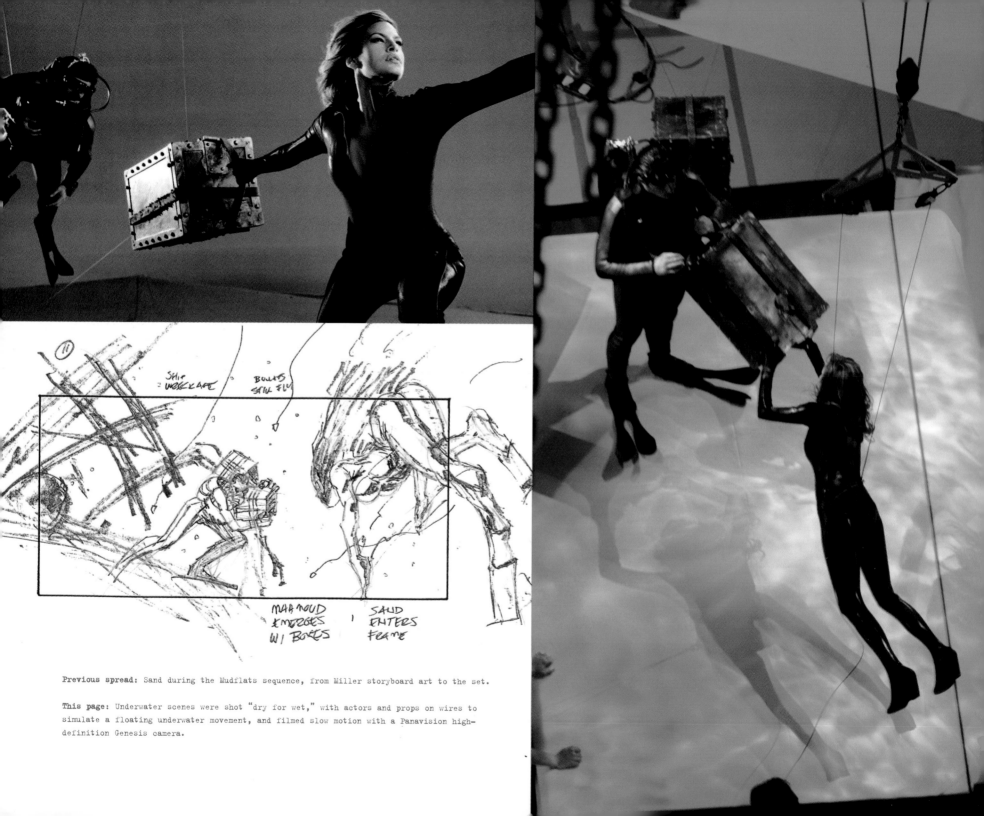

Previous spread: Sand during the Mudflats sequence, from Miller storyboard art to the set.

This page: Underwater scenes were shot "dry for wet," with actors and props on wires to simulate a floating underwater movement, and filmed slow motion with a Panavision high-definition Genesis camera.

About a month before filming was to begin, a core production team that included Miller, Deborah Del Prete, first assistant director Benita Allen, Stu Maschwitz, and Bill Pope met every day for hours, going through Miller's storyboards and discussing every aspect of principal photography. On September 18, the cast did a read-through at the place where the road to *The Spirit* began, Del Prete and Pritzker's Coronet Theatre. Soon after, on a flight to the soundstages in New Mexico to prepare for filming, Miller and Del Prete were still fine-tuning the screenplay, their in-flight discussion leading to two scenes Miller would work up, including an exchange between Dolan and his daughter which Del Prete considers one of the film's dramatic highlights.

All departments were integrated into the team concept. Stunt coordinator John Medlen prepared for his work by reading the script and breaking it down into the various action and stunt sequences, then met with Miller, Pope, and Maschwitz to discuss cinematography and end-game visual effects — "the whole team" was in on the discussions, Medlen noted.

Visual effects supervisor Stu Maschwitz would also serve as second unit director and work with Medlen and his crew. "My unit could have just done the squib hits and smoke passes and stuff that tends to earn a visual effects supervisor a second unit director credit," Maschwitz said. "But the fact that I got to do so much with the stunt team was a blast."

The Spirit was a "dream job" for prop master Randy Eriksen, who prepped five-to-six weeks before principal photography. His crew was basically himself and Chuck McSorley, his "right hand man," with local artist Fred Andrews doing work in New Mexico. A prop, which Eriksen

Above: Although underwater scenes were shot "dry for wet," a tank was used for shots where Sand emerges from the water.

defines as anything an actor touches or interacts with, could be made, bought, or found. Eriksen often went through Independent Studio Services (I.S.S.), a Los Angeles prop house, and when a designed prop needed to be made, he often called upon Studio Art Technology, the manufacturing arm of I.S.S.

"On greenscreen there's more importance on props, wardrobe, and make-up because that's really all you've got!" Eriksen noted. "You can't rely on the environment as much. Sometimes props can be minimal on a show, but not on *The Spirit*! This show was prop heavy. Frank and the whole vibe was super creative, it was like comic books for real life. The closer we could get to Will Eisner through Frank Miller's vision — that was it! Frank's assistant Xeroxed a lot of Eisner's old comics and they lifted things, like a street grate, straight out of the *Spirit* comics. When I look at Eisner's comics what jumps out is the character and style, like his manhole covers, streetlights, and old galvanized trashcans bent in the weirdest shapes, and we tried to do that.

"There's the standard stuff you find," Eriksen continued, "and there's weird stuff, like a giant cat food bag for feeding the Spirit's cats. Frank wanted a huge gunnysack-sized cat bag, with a hilarious graphic of a hissing cat, which I had made out of paper. For the wristwatch the Spirit wears, we looked at a hundred watches and Frank just happened to pick one from 1911, a plain old white-faced watch with a leather band that I got from Face Value Props, basically a guy who rents stuff out of his garage and specializes in old watches, eye glasses, and cameras."

When Sam Jackson wanted a monocle for his turn as a Nazi-inspired villain, Eriksen found a website devoted to monocles. For a scene in the Octopus's lair where the Spirit is tied up in a dentist's chair, the prop man got special soft rope at an "adult store." Many props were key story points, including the locket that bonds young lovers Denny and Sand. Eriksen obtained six versions of the locket, gold plating them and fitting photographs of the actors inside,

and aging one of the lockets to look like it had been underwater for years in the Mudflats where the adult Spirit finds this talisman of lost love.

Props and set pieces played an important part, given a major lesson The Orphanage learned on *Sin City* — *build* everything actors touch or interact with, rather than go to the time and expense of creating them with CG. The art department designed many of the physical elements, from floor and ground surfaces, to sidewalks and stairways, pier pylons and the Mudflats. But the literal interpretation of what actors interacted with changed during production, as set decorator Gabrielle Petrissans was asked to bring in more physical objects to dress the greenscreen sets.

"We tried to not have the methodology be the style," Maschwitz explained. "If there was an office with a wall behind someone, there was no reason to do that CG. If it was easy to put up a couple of flats and have a little set, that's what we'd do. I think we had more sets, and more detailed sets, than for my sequence on *Sin City*."

Miller storyboard art, Spirit and Octopus getting down and dirty in the
Mudflats (note the severed cop's head, which the Octopus uses as a
weapon).

One set piece Miller lobbied for was the revolving door of the Donenfeld Building, a dramatic Art Deco skyscraper that would otherwise be a computer generated creation. "In an early production meeting," Miller recalled, "I stopped everybody at the revolving doors and said, 'Look, I want to save money as much as anybody here, but sometimes you have to be lavish. I want the most beautiful revolving doors and they've got to be working, because I want to pull off shots that have never been done before.' And we've got a couple of revolving door shots that could only be done practically, but they could only have been done artificially as well. They're impossible angles looking down as the action takes place."

Left: The Octopus and Spirit face off.

Above: Associate visual effects supervisor Aaron Rhodes views a pre-production animatic.

Next spread and following: Miller storyboard art for the Mudflats sequence, with one directly Eisner-inspired shot.

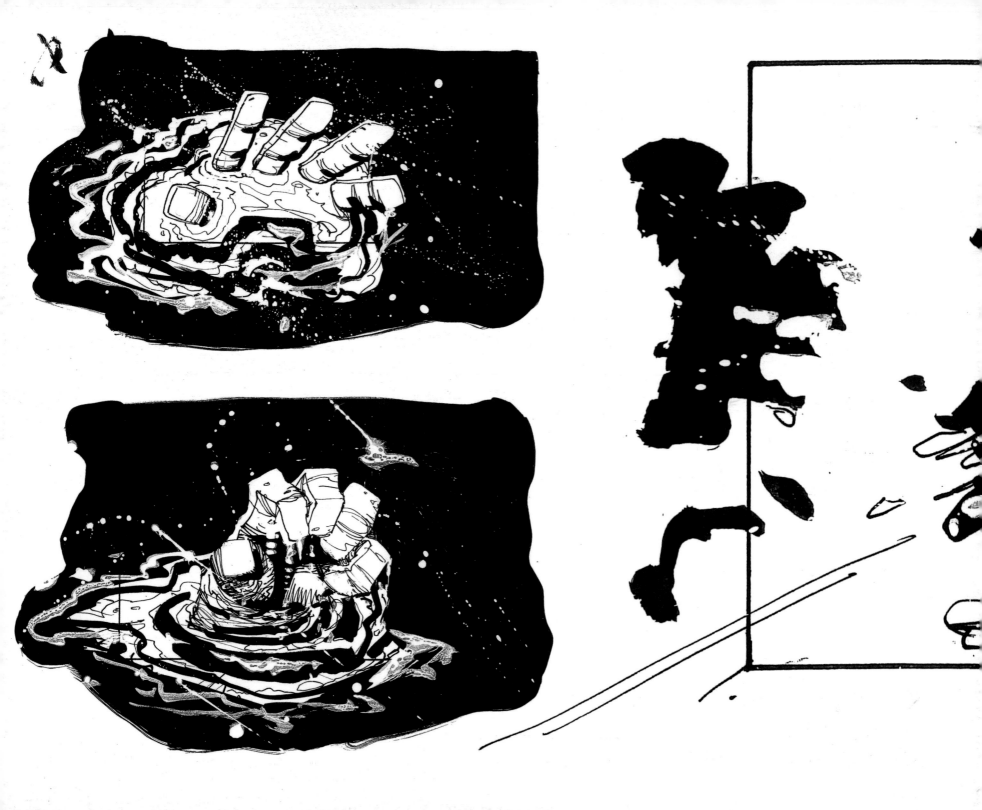

Miller's storyboards informed animatics that The Orphanage prepared for certain sequences several months before filming (animatics being low-resolution, 3-D computer graphics animation for scenes, prepared during the previsualization stage). "The boards were very telling, but needed translation," noted The Orphanage associate visual effects producer Aaron Rhodes. "We had three categories of previz shots. Category one: we slipped in a still frame drawn by Frank that told the whole story, like an establishing shot or a close-up of eyes. Second: compositors broke up [Miller's storyboards] into layers and moving parts using After Effects [commercial software] that we could animate in a 2.5-D style, just generating a little motion with the still frames. Category three: we had CG modelers and animators take the storyboards and bring them to life. All the storyboards were black and white, in that very *noir* and contrasty Frank look, so even the 3-D stuff we put through some toon shader processes [for the look of hand-drawn animation] to make it look high contrasty and similar to Frank's storyboards."

Animatics were done for complicated sequences, including the Mudflats, which featured a no-holds-barred battle between the Spirit and the Octopus in his Western bad guy regalia. "I was lucky enough to see the first part of the Mudflats animatics," Michael Dennison said, "because it dictated what the action would be and what the costumes had to do and didn't have to do, how much would be in silhouette, how much in light — all those things were extraordinarily educational. I knew the Octopus's costumes had to swoop and

Left: Miller storyboard art, Octopus in Mudflats, with Samuel Jackson in a final frame from the scene.

Right: Jackson in the outlandish cowboy hat and costume he wears at the Mudflats.

fly and float, not unlike the Spirit's trench coat. It was all about movement, catching the air and making visual miracles, juxtaposed with this very static brawl, fighting in the mud."

The animatics were Gabriel Macht's first taste of the look and feel of the upcoming production. "I didn't actually get Frank's storyboards until we started shooting in Albuquerque. [For the storyboards,] he basically took Eisner's drawings and sort of put his Frank Miller touch on it, which is a darker, more violent, rawer version of what Eisner did."

"Frank drew everything, that's how we got an indication of what this movie would look like," noted The Orphanage visual effects producer Nancy St. John. "What I thought was interesting was he would draw a lot of lines in pencil, detailing a scene — and then he'd black out whole sections. It was like he needed to lay everything out to see what really needed to be there to tell the story."

St. John, a veteran visual effects producer who had worked

at Industrial Light + Magic, put the challenge of supervising the visual effects in cold numbers — an estimated 1,911 visual effects shots. "I was at the point where I was tired of end-of-the-world movies, the world blowing up. I wanted to stay in visual effects, but veer off in a more artistic and graphical direction. When *The Spirit* came along, I was excited because it was not only an artistic challenge, but a challenge to me as a producer to balance out over 1,900 shots. This was beyond a doubt the most organized movie I've ever seen and a lot of the credit should go to Deb, and Frank Miller, who had a very clear vision of what he wanted to see."

Bill Pope, overseeing first and second units, would utilize the high-definition Genesis camera from Panavision. For underwater scenes, it was decided not to film underwater, but go "dry for wet," flying actors on wires to simulate swimming motions and shooting high-speed for the slow-motion effect of being underwater. "Digital slow motion has been a problem," Pope noted. "They've managed to get digital

Above and opposite: The Spirit is pulled toward Lorelei (Jaime King) in an underwater sequence, with the help of the wire rigs.

Next spread: Sand underwater, in a final shot and Miller storyboard art.

cameras to run sixty frames-per-second, but I was figuring on 400–1,000. I went to Google and what showed up was the Phantom camera. I tested a couple of other prototypes, but the Phantom was the one that was ready to be used."

A big advantage of digital cameras was their forty-minute tape capacity, instead of the typical ten-minute roll of film. "Working on tape, everybody works at a real clip and you keep your energy up," Miller said. "This film, as with most films, was shot out of sequence, and with a greenscreen world the actor's imagination had to be in play to imagine what might ultimately be surrounding them. People always joke about actors who spend all their time in their trailer — would that that were true for the actors' sakes! Actors *hate* sitting in trailers, they love to work. Could you imagine focusing on being somebody else, say your job was to be Robin Hood, and having to spend hours at a time out of character and then have to jump back into it? This wonderful method of working allows you a chance to never stop being Robin Hood."

THIS WAY,
PECKERWOOD!

THE SPIRIT

THE SPIRIT
MASKED CRUSADER

"I'M THE SPIRIT.
I BEAT UP BAD GUYS."

THE OCTOPUS

ARCH -ENEMY

"ALMOST NOTHING BEATS PULLING THE HEAD CLEAN OFF A COP!"

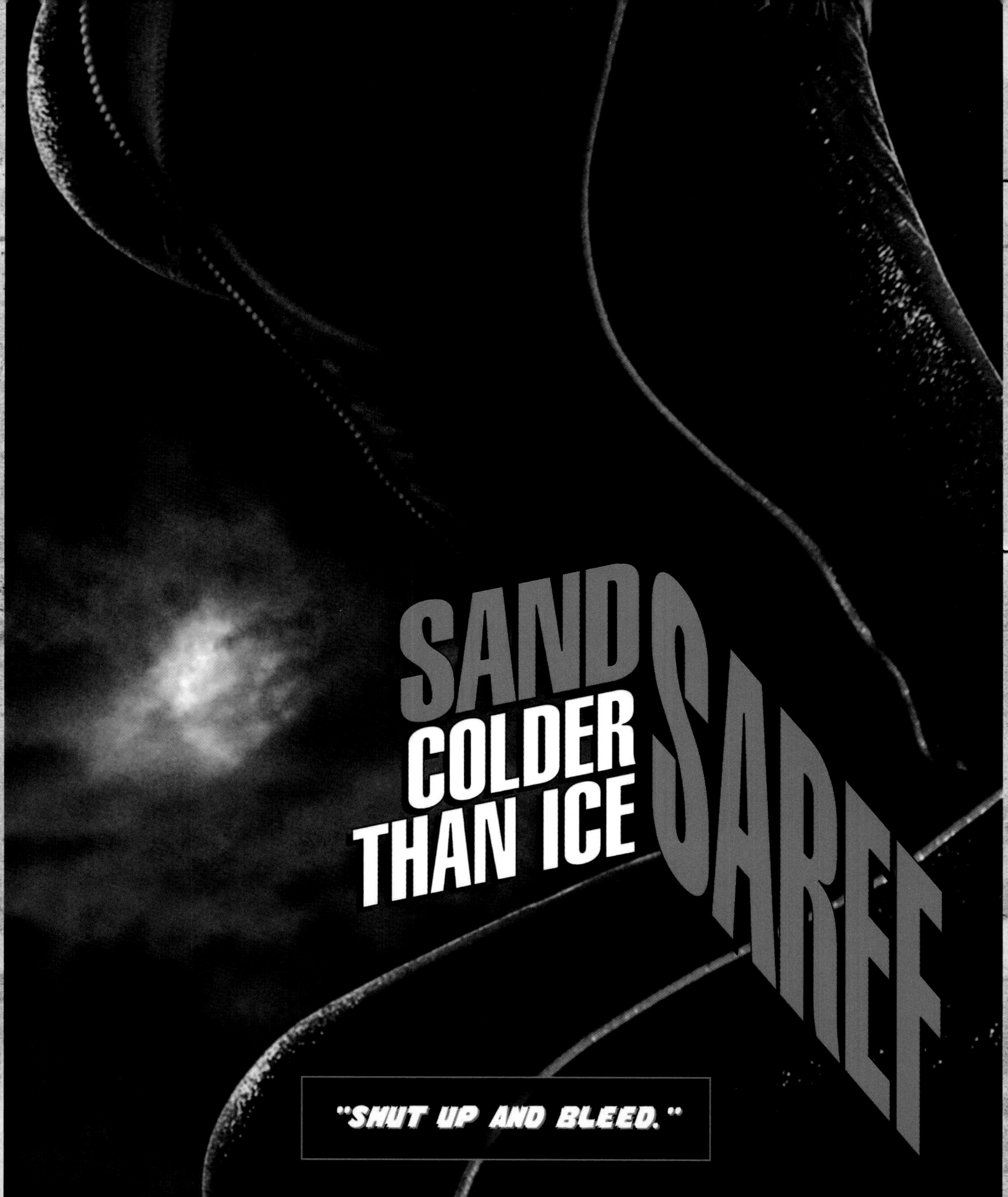

SAND SAREE

COLDER THAN ICE

"SHUT UP AND BLEED."

DR. ELLEN DOLAN

WHIP-SMART
GIRL NEXT DOOR

"I FEEL LIKE BREAKING ALL KINDS OF RULES..."

SILKEN FLOSS

FRIGID VIXEN

"THIS IS FUN."

PLASTER OF PARIS

MURDEROUS DANCER

"I WILL STICK TO MY MAN TILL DEATH DO US PART."

LORELEI ROX

THE ANGEL OF DEATH

"BE MINE. NOW AND FOREVER..."

THE GREEN
WORLD

"We were trying to strip things to their bare minimum — the goal was to do *Sin City* squared. This should be even more graphic than that. How far can we go? There was another thing pushing on us, besides that chip on our shoulder, and it's that Eisner was a very naturalistic drawer. There is a graphic side to Eisner, which is the part I think inspired Frank as a kid, but we also had to pay some homage to that naturalistic side. So we had those two things pushing and pulling on us."

BILL POPE

 lbuquerque Studios is not far from the airport, at the top of a mesa where shiny new soundstages sit in the middle of a vast, flat expanse. When *The Spirit* arrived in October of 2007, the studio was so new, so "way out there," as Maschwitz noted, the facility wasn't even on Google satellite maps.

"We were driving up to the studio and they were literally putting the signposts up," co-producer F.J. DeSanto recalled. "I spend half my time on studio lots, and this was bigger than anything I'd ever seen."

The Spirit was the first to use Stages 7 and 8, which were separated by elephant doors. In pre-production, Bill Pope and Benita Allen organized a layout that allowed first and second units to run simultaneously. The stages were divided into what the production called the "Green World," home to the main first-unit greenscreen area, and the "Black World," where stunts and wire work were staged against greenscreen, a practical Mudflats set was built for exterior shots, and sets were draped in black or elements shot against black. Monitors positioned all over the vast spaces allowed everyone to see what was being filmed at all times.

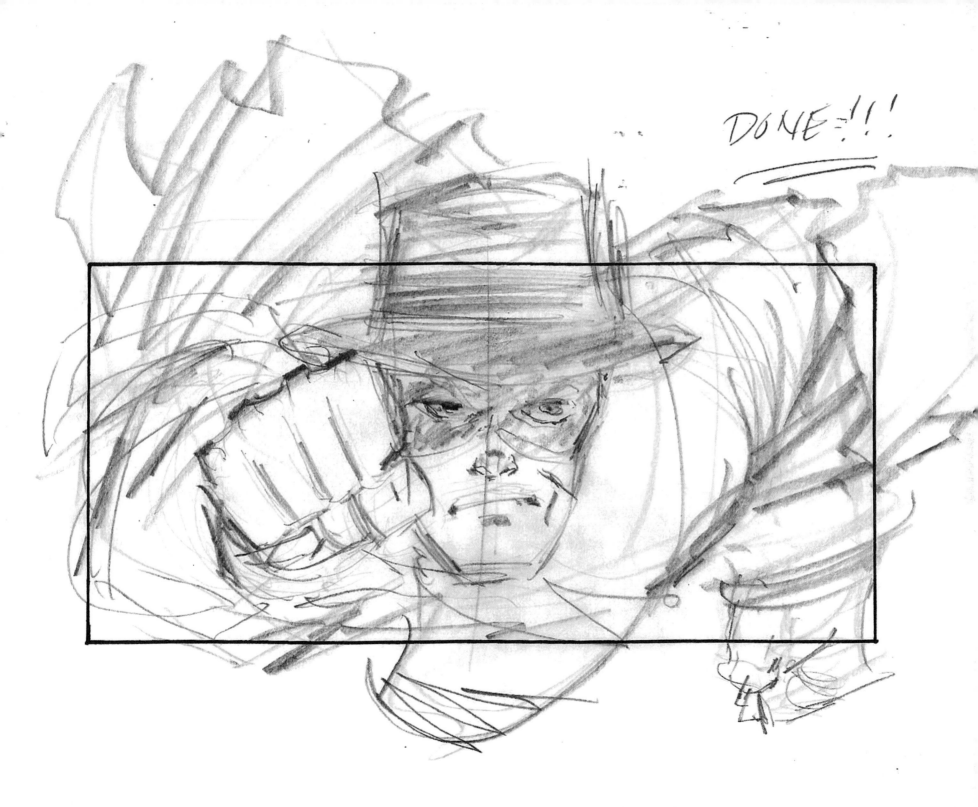

"Each day would be a new set of issues, but there was a consistency and pace," producer Pritzker said of the forty-eight-day shooting schedule. "It was like a real job, coming to work and not worrying about rain and all the issues you deal with on location. Each day always began at a big board where Frank's storyboards were put up so everybody could look at what sequences we'd be working on. That was the beauty of working with an artist — the entire movie was mapped out."

Eva Mendes for one did not like working on greenscreen — at first. By the end of principle photography she loved it, likening it to stage work. Indeed, the live theater "black box" principle of stripped down sets helped actors grasp the green void. "In a funny way, a greenscreen movie reminds me of designing for the theater," said art director Provenza, who studied at the Yale School of Drama. "A lot is not there, it mirrors the selective reality on the stage. Other than some elemental TV stuff with blue and greenscreen with video, I hadn't done an all-greenscreen production. It was very eye-opening."

"I'd never done anything against bluescreen or greenscreen," added Dan Lauria. "But whenever an actor learns their lines, and has a [mental] image of what a set is going to be, ninety-nine percent of the time when you get to the set it's nothing like you were picturing it. Well, with greenscreen, all I'm seeing is what I thought it would be! It was like working to the fourth wall of the theater in a play — out there it's anything you want it to be. I enjoyed that, it actually surprised me."

"I did three *Star Wars* movies, so I was sort of a veteran of the Big Green Room," Samuel Jackson said. "I didn't worry about there not being anything there. I let my imagination run to do the things I needed to do to create a reality of my own that they could draw around and do things to. It's a fun place to be, an actor's playground. I was an only child, so I spent a lot of time in my own room reading and creating stuff, so being in an empty space was perfect for me."[1]

Stunt coordinator Don Frazee admitted the greenscreen world was somewhat bewildering. Although he had worked on effects-filled productions, like *Pirates of the Caribbean: The Curse of the Black Pearl*, he hadn't worked on an all-greenscreen shoot. He had also been thrown into the fire, being called to work only four or five days before shooting began. "Originally, they didn't feel there would be a need for practical effects, but then they realized they'd need things like the wind and elements," Frazee recalled of the work he headed up with set foreman Scott Lingard. "So we were playing catch-up.

"I'm used to greenscreen, but based around a certain amount of reality. I've never worked on a project like this, because things didn't always seem to tie together. There'd be a scene shot for the Mudflats and then, a week later, a police car would be shot that would go into a corner of that scene. It was a lot of little elements, overlapping. Frank Miller did a good set of storyboards and that's how I kept track. But Stu and Frank had to stay in close communication about the elements they needed and how they would put them together."

Opposite: Stuntman Surels takes a fall and does a little heavy lifting — all in a day's work.

Above: Eva Mendes rehearses a stunt in the flying rig.

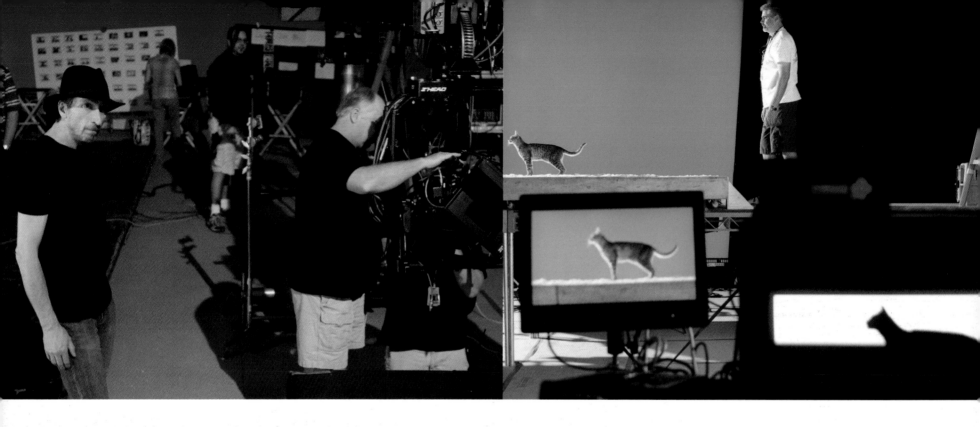

Gigi Pritzker observed that from the start Frank Miller created a "collaborative, yet decisive environment on set, two critical pieces for a director."

"I know how lucky and hard it is to win that battle [making a movie]," Miller explained. "But you can stop things from going wrong simply by projecting an aura of confidence in what you're after. It's a principle my father taught me, that people want to do good work and if you give them a clear objective they will surprise you with their magic. But if you dither and falter, they're going to sense that and work less hard. I've seen directors lose the confidence of actors and it becomes like a feeding frenzy, with actors suddenly ad libbing to beat the band. You have to have a strong sure hand, but also be flexible so these sparks of genius will happen and you can go, 'Yeah. Course

correction, five percent.' And be smart enough to turn."

The core team concept, which emerged during pre-production, flourished during the collaborative work of production. "The obvious precedent was *Sin City*, which had the all-encompassing vision of Robert Rodriguez, who acted as his own DP [director of photography] and visual effects supervisor," Maschwitz noted. "We were trying to take that to the next step, but instead of one person wearing all those hats, we had this visual triumvirate of Frank, Bill, and myself. Our direct collaboration was pretty much implementation/methodology. We'd have larger conversations leading up to specifics of whether we should shoot greenscreen or black, what was the best way to capture an image? Bill and I were keenly interested in finding new ways of getting Frank's vision on the screen.

Miller storyboard art, Spirit sneaks up on sniper.

"If you look at Frank's artwork, there's often strong silhouettes," Maschwitz continued. "You might have a night scene, but it'd be a black building silhouetted in front of white, basically a blank page. So I would have talks with Bill about how to put that image on the screen. If it's night, and it's snowing, you don't put any lights in front, but put a gigantic light behind a building and light up the sky to a point where if not white, it's certainly brighter than fifty percent gray, and you've pretty much made that image. In CG, you don't have to follow that rule book, you can just make the sky white. But I preferred to emulate the photographic approach and make our CG backgrounds look like we obeyed the rules of practical sets and locations and photography and lights."

Many productions had moved towards greenscreen and away from the formerly ubiquitous bluescreen as a better medium for isolating live-action and digitally layering in backgrounds. "There are three color channels — red, green, and blue — and each has a variation on their fidelity," explained Aaron Rhodes. "Green has the least amount of grain in it, the blue color channel has the most grain or 'noise.' So if you try to pull a color key with bluescreen, your edges are going to be a little more noisy and grainy, but when you remove greenscreen, the key will be much sharper."

With visual effects supervisor Maschwitz often pulled away from first unit to direct second unit, Rhodes was his eyes and ears in the Green World — "Stu Two," Deborah Del Prete dubbed him. The visual effects team had a host of concerns dictating whether something would be staged in the Green World or Black World. "It was kind of a constant battle to let everyone on set understand why we were doing greenscreen in certain places, or black in others — it was tricky for *us* to figure out at times," Rhodes said. "There were principles we talked about before shooting that we stuck with, like having to shoot in front of black, as opposed to green, if it was going to be a black scene."

A scene designed for Eisner-esque shadow only needed a

black-draped set, which made for "fluidity," Rhodes noted, because that set wouldn't need a computer generated background, it could be shot and done. But when actors had to fire guns, they did so in front of black backing, which better allowed for isolation of the brightness from the muzzle flash and smoke. "But things changed on a day-to-day basis," Rhodes added. "We'd move with the groove when we needed to."

There were known quantities of physical sets and props, but before a shot Miller, his actors, and the production team would "start walking and talking and blocking," Pope explained, orienting everyone as to what was out there in the greenscreen void. Sometimes the director just drew a picture.

"Pictures are instant communication," Pope said. "'What the hell is this scene about, Frank?' He'd say, 'It's this beat right here.' And he'd sit down and draw a work of art in front of you that made your hair stand up on the back of your neck. He'd draw, literally, almost as fast as I can say it. It's spooky how fast he can draw. With a few simple lines he can suggest an entire scene, and that's invaluable. He can distill anything into pure Frank Miller. It's really exciting, actually."

Maschwitz described how Pope often came over to him with "a glimmer in his eye," which meant a Big Idea was brewing and he wanted to see how it might or might not work with visual effects and color timing. Pope recalled one example: a scene where Ellen Dolan struggles to save a dying man's life. "I was always trying to play with single light sources as much as possible, and in the scene with Ellen the sources of light were cop cars stopped along the moors with their headlights on, basically one single raking hot light source. Cops are milling around, she is in the background. I proposed having someone stand in the light, while she and her assistant are in the dark, pure silhouettes. When she had a line, she could lean over the body and into the light, say her line, and lean back into the dark and become a silhouette again. It was just playful. Frank is very playful with all his elements, so he inspires you to be just as playful."

Stu Maschwitz calls it "greenscreen psychosis" — filmmakers see so much green background that they need to fill in later they start thinking *anything* is possible. "There's a leap of faith that comes with these movies," Maschwitz acknowledged. "I tried to mitigate that as much as possible, and give Frank the experience he should have as a director, by seeing images on the monitor which were what his movie was going to look like."

That final look would include flashback scenes of young Denny and Sand cast in a honeyed sepia tone, scenes emulating Miller's distinctive silhouette style, and sometimes color elements popping out of desaturated-looking backgrounds, notably the Spirit's blood-red tie (a graphic effect, Maschwitz says, that was a rare departure from the photographic-based approach). As it was on *Sin City*, and far in advance of the post-production color correction process, Maschwitz and Pope designed a series of LUTs ("Look Up Tables"), color corrections approximating the final color scheme which could be applied to scenes as they were being shot and shown, real-time, on a special monitor.

Visual effects producer Nancy St. John says that during the fifty days of filming she basically "lived in a little black tent in the big green room with the digital camera assistant."

One monitor showed the raw greenscreen shot on the Genesis camera, another could show the application of a specific LUT. Although the color correction applied only to what was physically on set, the distracting bright green backgrounds could be replaced with a neutral gray. The footage with LUTs applied was what Miller and Del Prete looked at when they approved the day's work. "Every single shot in this movie had an LUT that had to be applied and which would be processed through our Digital Intermediate [DI] suite [at The Orphanage]," Nancy St. John explained of their post-production digital color correction system.

"In most movies, I'm the only person who knows what the movie is going to look like because I'm going to be [color] timing it at the end," Bill Pope noted. "On this one, everybody knew — it was on the screen. Anybody could walk into the tent and see what a scene would look like, absent the backgrounds. It was a handful of LUTs for the whole movie and there'd be a discussion and we'd choose them as we went along. One look might be super contrasty, which would work for an action scene — that might be Look Up Table One. There could be another LUT where colors were super vibrant, or an LUT where anything lit by a fluorescent light glowed red."

The color correction proved to be Pope's least favorite aspect of shooting digital. "I did like things in the digital realm, but what's bad is you're not at the camera. The DP has to be in the black tent with monitors, that's the only way you can control and even *see* your colors and what the lighting is like. If I went into the black tent I could see what it looked like after the LUT was applied, but if I stood next to the camera, I couldn't see it. The camera does not feed the look you're after back into the eyepiece. To spend my day inside a tent is not cinematography to me. I like to do the camera movement, so [there was a lot of back and forth between filming and the tent]. That was awkward

and cumbersome. But there's a look specific to Frank and the *Sin City* thing, so it was okay."

The next step of detailing the backgrounds was low-tech — Maschwitz and Pope simply drew pictures on paper, with Miller giving final approvals and often contributing his own sketches. "It's not Future World," Pope laughed, "we were just staring at a [monitor] wondering what the heck was in that sea of gray — it might be water with a ship passing, or fog rolling in, a light source coming from here or there. We'd draw a quick sketch, stick it in an envelope and send it off to The Orphanage — it's the same damn thing they did in 1945!"

Opposite: The elaborate elevated train set piece.

Above: Make-up artist Elaine Offers applies final touches to Eva Mendes.

Next page: Miller storyboard art, Spirit swims towards a taunting Lorelei.

Ultimately, all departments were mindful that their work was inextricably tied to post-production visual effects and color timing. "I knew that with greenscreen, we'd be more of an assistance to visual effects," special effects coordinator Frazee noted. "All our practical elements, Stu would take into CG. We'd do ten squib hits and he'd replicate them into fifty. Or we'd dress a lot of sets with paper snow, and have blowers acting like wind blowing it around, and Stu would take that further."

Make-up department head Isabel Harkins had concerns as to how her work would be affected by Pope's lighting and The Orphanage's subsequent color correction work. "They were going to pull out all the warm colors and [selectively choose] reds, but the girls wanted to be glamorous, and they like warm colors. Most films, to make things softer [for women], use diffusion through lenses and filters, but on this show, the diffusion was put on at the end by The Orphanage. So, during filming, I consulted with Stu and the DP to calibrate for the end result, and we did testing the first couple of weeks. It might have looked crazy to the eye, but [the make-up] was designed so by the time it was translated to the final film, they'd still look good — to give a kind of sinister look Frank was after without making people look like monsters. The tough part was communicating to the actors that it would all translate really well later on. It was tricky, a tremendous amount of trust. A lot of scenes with Paz Vega had a red light behind her, which can turn things black. She's angular in her face, so I had to take her natural shading out to be able to compensate for what the light and treatment was going to do, because she wanted to be beautiful and soft."

Harkins, who credits mime artist Marcel Marceau as an inspiration and was drawn to make-up for its inherent "magic," discovered the production's comic book aesthetic worked in her favor. "Frank Miller is so graphic, so you could emphasize a graphic look, to mime the cartoon [aesthetic] with real make-up, which is what the film is all about.

We could transform Dolan, for example, to look like the comics character, but with painting, not prosthetics. It was a lot of shading and highlights and contrasts, very flat make-up, like old theater make-up. Shading is you go into places to create a sinking, hollow effect, to create a contrast. Just as an artist draws black lines on a white, flat surface, you create, like a drawing, the look of comics on people. That was exciting."

In addition to having actors look like comics characters, one of Miller's ground rules was they had to move like them, too, especially the Spirit. This was of particular importance to stunt coordinator John Medlen and to Stu Maschwitz's work as second unit director. "One of the things I'm most proud of on this movie is we didn't have a digital stunt double for the Spirit," Maschwitz said. "We had a lot of really inventive stunt rigging, with a quarter of one stage devoted to a stunt gantry that could have multiple wired stunt performers doing difficult things. Between John Medlen, David Hugghins — who built an amazing, all-purpose stunt truss — and Ronn Surels, the stunt double for the Spirit, I was in the lap of luxury."

Previous page: A trussed-up Spirit awaits Plaster's entrance.

This page: Plaster and the tools of her trade.

Opposite: In the Octopus's lair, Plaster does her deadly dance before a helpless Spirit.

This page and previous spreads: Ronn Surels races across the rooftops of Central City. The silhouette image, a signature look in Frank Miller's graphic novels, was one of the film's graphic motifs.

During a prep period a month before principal photography, Medlen and his team rehearsed and videotaped as many of the stunts as possible, in the process perfecting the Spirit's distinctive style which they would match to Spirit poses Miller had struck in the day's storyboards. "The Spirit's style had to fit within a stunt, it was more than choreography," Medlen explained. "It wasn't just a fight scene, it was about giving the Spirit a pose. We had to define his style, his stance, his walk, and his attitude, as well as the action."

The Spirit's exaggerated fighting pose had his shoulders back and arms out so the character's distinctive movements could be clearly and graphically delineated in shadow and silhouette. "For combat scenes, I told the actors to respect gravity," Miller explained. "I said, 'I want the Spirit to be so strong that when he hits people they fall straight down.' If someone is shot or punched, they don't fly twenty feet — they *drop*. The power of a punch is contained if the character drops, it's released if they fly, it's actually less energy. You *destroy* someone if you hit them and they fall straight down."

Once a pose was figured out, a specific rig was selected. One gag pulled the Spirit up to camera to produce the optical illusion of falling. "We had the Spirit dive down at us, like he's coming off of his fist," Medlen explained.

Above: Miller storyboard art, Spirit treads a power line.

Next spread: Miller storyboard art, Spirit smackdown.

"We put the camera up high, had the Spirit facing upwards as if he's Superman jumping towards the sky, and pulled him on a ratchet, a system using compressed air fired at 300 or 400 [pounds per square inch]. He'd go flying at thirty-five miles per hour, whizzing by the camera to give that real effect of falling. We used a lot of ratchets on this show."

Medlen estimated it was forty feet to the ceiling, with the truss system set at thirty feet and capable of flying performers in all three axes of motion. Once a performer was wired, the controller on the ground could move them like a puppet on strings. "It was a rectangular truss and pulley system where we could maneuver the pick point anywhere, like you're floating on air, going in circles, or up and down," Medlen said. "My stunt riggers could control it in various ways. Sometimes they used a winch system or a pulley system, a wheel, sometimes it was a motorized device that moved it from one place to another."

Nylon harnesses were custom fit to the actors, with pick points for the wires that went through the fabric of their costumes. Lycra cables were used, which were softer and easier to handle than steel cables, particularly when a flip might cause skin to brush up against them. The cables were tested and rated for specific pounds of pressure but, to be safe, if Medlen and his team calculated a wire stunt at five hundred pounds of pressure, they'd go to cable rated for five thousand pounds.

Although the film's stars did a lot of their own stunts and wire work, stuntmen stepped in for the most difficult assignments. In Medlen's world, Spirit stuntman Ronn Surels was a "specialty guy," well-versed in martial arts for fighting stunts, but also a good "ground pounder" who could take a fall, and excellent at wire work. For a scene where the Spirit had to run and leap across the top of a building, Medlen decided it would be quicker to not rig and fly Macht, but simply have Surels, in full Spirit costume, leap off a twenty-five-foot high platform to a padded fall.

"Frank had a vision of the Spirit's non-superhero hero-ness," Maschwitz said. "The Spirit doesn't have a disposable income or bat-belt like Batman, he's just got his Converse All-Stars and a tactile, imperfect relationship with the city. Sometimes he jumps on a chimney and a brick falls off, but he always kind of makes it. There's a physicality to that, instead of him leaping around like a weightless CG character."

Whenever Miller needed a physical object or set piece, art director Rosario Provenza and assistant art director Todd Holland were assigned to design it to the director's satisfaction, with construction coordinator Robin Blagg building it. A case in point was the revolving door for the Donenfeld Building. The freestanding object was designed on a pivot mechanism that turned from the bottom, and which could be stopped off-camera by a hand brake. The art department worked out the details of fabrication with the construction coordinator to have most of the weight of the apparatus and turning mechanism be under a two-step

platform. "We had a contractor fabricate the steel work to our specs," Provenza said, "and when that was in place we built the skin around it, a fine grain hardwood we could paint to make it look bronze. There was supposed to be a marble floor around it, but I remembered an art director buddy of mine saying, 'When you're in a pinch, use Formica.' That's exactly what we used to create the revolving door platform, which was laminated and popped into place like a jigsaw puzzle piece."

One of the signature *Spirit* comics images, dubbed "the Eisner grate," was inspired by an Eisner splash page perspective view of the Spirit walking on a sidewalk as water flowed down the gutter, carrying letters spelling S-P-I-R-I-T to a foreground grate where a copy of a damp newspaper ends with, "Crime is a man-made stream." The grate was integrated into a cobblestones set piece drawn up by Holland for a scene of Spirit and Plaster of Paris, an old flame, escaping the Octopus through the sewer system and coming up to street level. The shot required a sixteen by twenty-four foot section of cobblestones built in three sections and elevated almost six feet above the stage floor, which allowed the camera to simulate a street level view as the Spirit pushed through the grate, for which Provenza designed a lip on the mortar so the shoving action dislodged old bricks and stone powder.

The cobblestones, purchased from a salvage yard, were also used to build a forty by thirty foot street section. Moveable sidewalks, pushed around on casters, were designed to indicate a particular area of town, with cracked sidewalks for more downtrodden sections of Central City. "We had a local plasterer from Albuquerque named Javier Fuentes who was on his first movie but performed magic with the masonry mixture for the sidewalks," Provenza noted. "When we wanted sidewalks with cracks, he put strings in the mixture and, just before it dried, pulled the string out, which created a crack effect."

The Mudflats was "a big, waterproof mattress," Provenza explained, a trough eight inches deep, lined and laid over with foam so performers wouldn't injure themselves, particularly in the big Spirit and Octopus face-off. Special effects head Frazee built both the twenty by forty foot Mudflats set and a fifteen by fifteen foot tank with muddy colored water for shots of actors seen entering the water (with the actual underwater scenes shot dry for wet). For the actual mud effect for the main Mudflats tank, Frazee trucked in containers of the edible "food thickener that's the basis for every movie goop," noted Maschwitz. The trashy estuary itself would be full of found or made items from prop man Randy Eriksen and set decorator Gabrielle Petrissans, from an old baby carriage Miller requested to tailpipes and the detritus of industrial waste.

In the early Mudflats sequence, the main characters converge as the Octopus and Sand race to find a buried treasure, and the Spirit arrives in time to fight his nemesis. In their battle, Octopus pulls a toilet from the muck and bashes it over the Spirit's head (a prop delivered by Eriksen from a mold made at Studio Art Technology). Another found object weapon, and one of the most celebrated props, was simply described in the script as a "lug wrench." It took form with a Miller silhouette drawing, which Eriksen detailed to look like steel and castiron. What Eriksen didn't appreciate initially was the *size* Miller wanted. "I made a foam mock-up that was four feet long, and Frank said, 'Oh no, no — *twice* that size!' So we made it seven feet long. Frank loved it, of course. It was so much fun working with Frank because he's so creative and over-the-top. It kind of opened me up and the more I did the more I loved it. It was a comic book mentality. We made several versions of the wrench, from lightweight to a really heavy one with a piece of steel in it for a scene where the Spirit has to run up it."

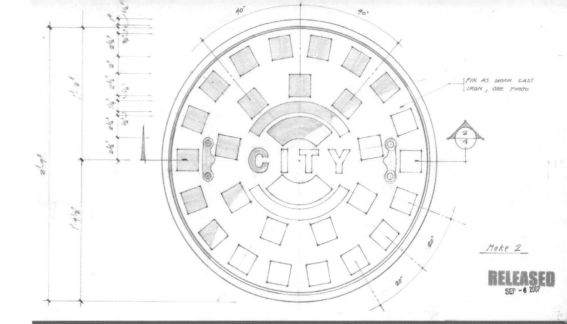

Previous spread: Construction plans and the final onscreen result of a showcase set piece: the Art Deco revolving door entryway to the Donenfeld Building, and the onscreen version of the iconic Eisner grate.

Opposite: Stunt coordinator John Medlen rehearses a manhole tossing stunt with Macht.

Above and below: Manhole cover design and final prop from Hand Prop Room. Prop man Eriksen crafted an Eisner-esque design inspired by old, tire-worn manhole covers. Multiples were made, from a heavy one cars could drive over to a lightweight version that gets thrown like a discus during a fight.

In the scene, the Octopus swings the gigantic wrench at the Spirit, misses, and as it's stuck in the muck, the Spirit runs up the wrench and kicks Octopus. For that shot, stuntmen took over, with wires rigged to Spirit stunt double Surels to hold him upright as he ran up the slippery prop. A line concealed in his back went straight up to a pulley that ran horizontally to another pulley some twenty feet away and under which Medlen was standing, positioned to control the rig. "I had the line in my hand, and I was moving with him," Medlen said. "I pulled the wire to take his weight off and lift as he leapt and kicked in the air. I pulled to give him more height and that little bit of superhuman strength. As he came down, I released enough to let him land on his feet. It requires knowing the mechanics of the body when someone is going to jump, when to pull, when they're landing, how much to give them and take the weight off their legs."

Gabrielle Petrissans, who explains her job as "being responsible for content and context in terms of story and character," found the demand for physical details increased as filming went on. "Defining the parameters of where CG stops and set decoration begins was tricky in the beginning. CG movies are new and CG movies and set decorating are really new! At first, Stu and Frank were saying it was whatever an actor touched or interacted with — but those parameters kind of got blown the first five or six days into principle photography. A lot of that came from Frank, stuff he was asking for. As we went on, it started to reveal itself."

The set decorator prepared boards with photographs of objects collected for the various sets, with options for the director. Miller, without hesitation, always picked the pieces he wanted, Petrissans recalled. "He *never* hesitated! I've worked with no one like Frank. A lot of production designers go with how something looks. He goes with how something makes him *feel*. After a few weeks with Frank, I realized I had to go with my gut, because that's what Frank was doing."

For *The Spirit* that meant anything that struck Petrissans as

Opposite, and previous spreads: The battle in the Mudflats included an old toilet and a gigantic wrench, which Octopus delivers where it hurts.

Left: The Mudflats wrench prop was of cartoonish proportions — grip Mike Lucero provides a scale comparison.

"creepy." Miller's directive from their L.A. interview meeting — "scare me" — inspired set pieces from a strange porcelain doll that dressed an alleyway to a "rib spreader" medical device Miller specifically requested for "The World Below," as the underground laboratory of the Octopus was known, to a two-foot diameter light fixture for the villain's lair fabricated from a cryogenic chamber (a "creepy science," Petrissans notes) found in a surplus store in Los Alamos.

The set decoration department often had to spring into action at a moment's notice — "this was the fire drill show," Petrissans said. There was, for instance, the early morning phone call requesting a desk for Silken Floss to sit on. Petrissans was at an Albuquerque antique shop when it opened at 10:00 a.m. and instantly saw what she wanted — a circa 1880s desk from Portugal. Within the hour, arrangements were made to rent and truck it to the shooting stage. "I walked right into it, that was Kismet! But we did a lot of gut feeling on this show."

The World Below, the Octopus's subterranean lair and laboratory, was an example of how original barebones sets transmuted into something more elaborate. The lab was planned to have a table, chair, and a beaker, but ended up with almost 400 pieces, by Petrissans' estimate. "If it gave me a creepy feeling, it worked, like a 1940s sterilizer for sterilizing instruments I got from Alpha Med [prop house] in Los Angeles. Frank wanted to see a mad scientist's lab. In fact, he came in on a Sunday and helped us dress that set."

The process of set decorating was like painting, first roughing in basic shapes with the major pieces, such as tables upon which things would sit, and then detailing in layers. "You keep layering until it starts to breathe, to look like what it's supposed to be," Petrissans explained. "That's the moment I look for, when it breathes, when you don't question its existence."

While the Spirit meets adversity with his fists, the Octopus has no compunction about using lethal force, from

exotic weapons—including six-inch diameter throwing stars Eriksen designed in an eight-legged octopus shape — to his favored guns, for which The Orphanage figured out a signature look. "When Sam Jackson was shooting his guns, we had a red and blue gel light on either side of him," Aaron Rhodes said. "We did that to isolate, in post-production, the red channel and see the left side of Sam illuminated, and then switch to the blue channel and see the right side of Sam illuminated. That was a cool gag Stu thought a lot about, so we could make and control those flashes coming out of his guns."

Randy Eriksen had a small armory of guns on set to serve the Octopus's every need. A gag in the final battle, as the Spirit and Dolan's police force move in on the Octopus, was that the villain would fire away with a gun in each hand until empty, then toss them away and pick up another, bigger set of guns. The "crazy progression," as Eriksen put it, began with a .50 caliber Desert Eagle, a real chrome gun with ivory handles which he got from the Independent Studio Services prop house.

Opposite: Originally planned to be virtually all greenscreen, the Octopus's subterranean lab ended up a set dresser's dream.

Above: Silken Floss gets in touch with her inner-Hitler.

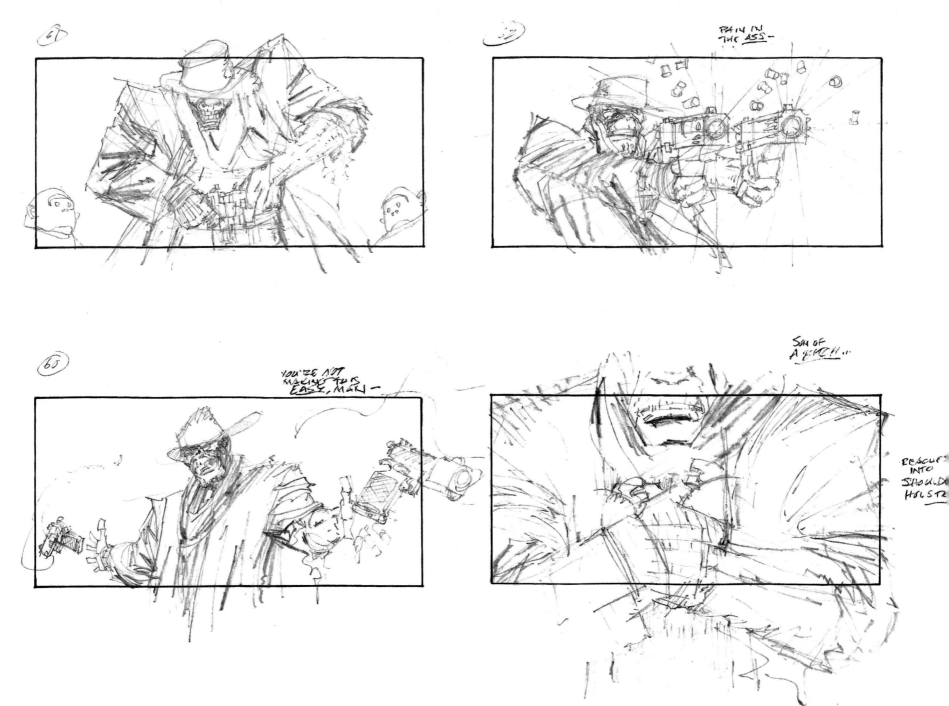

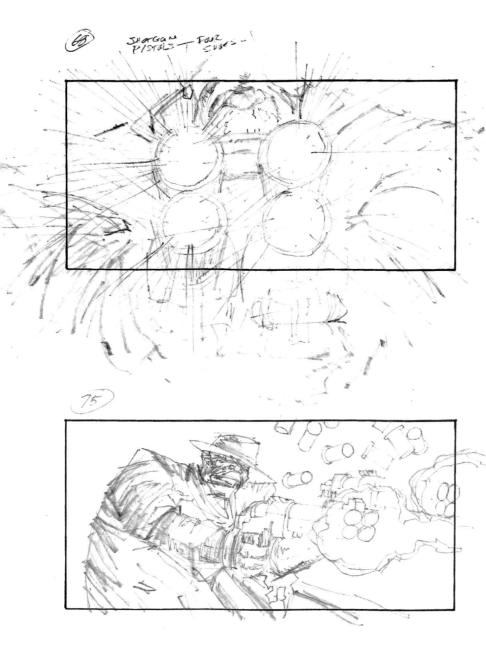

Opposite and above: Miller storyboard art, Octopus gunplay.

Right: Final frames from the scene.

An arsenal fit for an Octopus.

Anticlockwise from top: Shotgun pistol, Desert Eagle pistol, the .50 caliber Shark.

Opposite: The prop team assembles the Octopus's ultimate gun, The Darrow.

The next gun had to be bigger, so Eriksen designed a .50 caliber revolver he called The Shark, that was designed to look cartoony, with an oval-shaped barrel — a shape so unusual he had to go back a few times to Studio Art Technology to make sure they got it right. "The Shark was perfectly polished and we had it machined out of aluminum, and you'd think oval bullets would come out of it," Eriksen said. "It was beautiful and very over-the-top and shot .50 caliber blanks.

"The next was a short, four-barreled shotgun we ended up buying through the prop house, and we started cutting it down. Frank kept saying, 'Cut it down a little more!' So we cut most of the stock off, kept whittling this thing down, so it looked like a big pistol, over and under, the barrels are not side by side. Of course, it wasn't a real gun and couldn't even fire blank ammo like the other guns. So we had the special effects department rig them with squibs, so they did a blast, like a spark and smoke hit coming out. I was doing my prep work at the time in Los Angeles and Bill Pope was prepping in New Mexico, but I'd e-mail him photographs of the gun and he could envision looking at it through a lens just from seeing the still photograph. Bill was great, he shot right down the barrel of that thing."

During filming of the climactic battle, Jackson would toss each model of gun off-camera where Eriksen and his assistant, Chuck McSorley, caught them with furniture pads. When the four-barreled shotguns were spent, Jackson suddenly posed a question, Eriksen recalls: "Sam said, 'You can't just end it with a four-barrel, don't you got a *really big* gun!?'"

"Everybody on the set froze," Miller said. "I told them to bring out all the guns they had, because no one gun would do it. I stacked them together and Randy was wiring them and adding his pieces, and in moments Samuel was welding these uncanny things that could be lifted but looked utterly preposterous and fantastic, like a Transformer robot. That was one of my favorite moments on the picture."

The mega-gun was nicknamed The Darrow in honor of

comics artist Geof Darrow, whose work on *Hard Boiled*, a 1990 Dark Horse mini-series written by Miller, featured a gun-toting main character. "What I had on hand were a bunch of cheap plastic replicas of SWAT rifles, actually paint-ball guns, but wholly realistic, lightweight, and painted flat black," Eriksen recalled. "We ended up Zip-tying them together and I think we had two rifles and a grenade launcher and we put some shotgun shell blanks on the outside of it — they were like four guns in each hand that he could hold up and pretend to fire. The Darrow was just a last-minute idea Sam and Frank had on the set and we did on the fly. Frank was saying, 'Oh, my God, this is great!' As I was taking all our SWAT guns and strapping them together, I remember thinking, 'I don't know if this is embarrassing or genius!' Crazy. But that was Frank Miller, that was working on *The Spirit*."

When principal photography wrapped on schedule, the show was over for most departments. But for Miller, Del Prete, and The Orphanage, things were heating up. Post-production began in the Odd Lot editing suites in Los Angeles, where another critical team member, editor Greg Nussbaum, joined them. Greg came to the film after being recommended by Stu Maschwitz, with whom he'd worked on commercials and music videos. "The difficulty with this type of film is that your editor only has actors on green screen to cut. They really have to have a lot of imagination to understand what they are doing. Deborah wanted someone who would really understand Frank's style like the rest of the team. Greg had been an editor for the pre-viz period of *The Spirit* and I knew he was very talented and would be a good match," recalled Stu Maschwitz. Del Prete gave the first few weeks' footage to Nussbaum as a test to see what he would make of it. She and Miller loved the results and brought him on board.

The so-called "director's cut" period began towards the end of January of 2008, with an extra two-to-three weeks before March 28, the target date at which all edited footage was to be turned over to The Orphanage. "We shoot actors on set, and

then spend months and months with them [in editing]," Del Prete said. "You're looking at every little nuance in their faces; you're intimately involved with them all over again."

Deborah Del Prete recalls a Lionsgate executive asked how they could possibly cut the movie without knowing what the backgrounds would be. It was a principle Miller was familiar with as a graphic novelist. "I did a series of graphic novels with [colorist] Lynn Varley where it was my job to often provide just a third or a quarter of the image, and often I didn't know what she'd do with the rest of it, beyond a general notion. For me to know there's going to be a thunderhead [behind a foreground image] is perfectly normal, because I was in her sure hands so often. With Stu, I'd constantly be going to Bill and saying, 'Can we give Stu a little more room on this? I want to see something really big back there!'"

As Michel Dennison observed, "This idea evolved to make sure you were in synch with what Frank and the effects people had in mind and what they were ultimately going to put in the background, because their process started after the initial filming. It was wonderful because you're imagining everything, it's this incredible imagination game, you know?"

Post is one of the most important parts of the process — especially in a film like *The Spirit* — and while they had Stu Maschwitz and The Orphanage making sure every visual was perfect, Frank and Deborah also had to ensure the sound and music was up to the same standard. They spent a lot of time listening to scores and meeting with composers. "We were very fortunate to have a wealth of choices," Del Prete said. "After seeing a sample of the footage literally everyone we wanted to meet with was very excited about taking on the film. The hardest part was having to say no to so many really great music makers." After consideration, the highly accomplished multiple Academy Award-nominated David Newman — the composer of the scores for *Anastasia*, *Ice Age* and *The Phantom* among many others — joined the team. "Frank wanted elements of the 1940s jazz sound married with iconic heroic music, and even a touch of the Spaghetti Western," Del Prete said. "David was able to bring it all home for us."

"*Sin City* was a dream project, but really a prelude to *The Spirit*. Odd Lot basically said to us, 'We want you to do what you've been talking about and dabbling in this whole time on *Sin City*, we want to put you in charge of designing that work flow for an entire movie — put your money where your mouth is!' Okay, that was what I was talking about and now it was time to do it. So I came into this with guns ablazing."

STU MASCHWITZ

he Presidio of San Francisco sits at the hilly northern tip of the city, a strategic spot spanning ocean to bay that made it a military stronghold for two hundred years. The National Park Service, not the Army, now runs the place. The parade grounds of the Main Post retains the basic orientation from when Spain first established its military presence here, but barracks and buildings house a variety of tenants. In the former Fourth U.S. Army Headquarters is the San Francisco Film Centre, which includes The Orphanage. *The Spirit* team itself was quartered in an underground level, behind a pass-code safe door, in a place they called the Bunker. It was also called Central City for the effects unit's designation as a separate entity within The Orphanage. Central City was a huge "I/O" — In and Out — the hub for receiving edited footage from Odd Lot, then out-sourcing and receiving back work from such visual effects vendors as The Orphanage itself, Fuel in Sydney, Ollin in Mexico City, Digital Dimension in Montreal, Cinesoup in Santa Barbara, and a number of Los Angeles houses: Furious FX, Look Effects, Riot.

To put the work in perspective, producer Nancy St. John noted that in the early 1990s, at the dawn of the digital age when she managed the computer graphics group at ILM, *Terminator 2* presented an incredible challenge at fifty-to-fifty-four visual effects shots — *The Spirit* had 1,911 shots. Within a tight six-month post-production period, the Central City unit had to bid and award all those shots, incorporate feedback from the director and producer, make sure all delivered finals looked good at 2K resolution (two thousand pixels across, standard high resolution for film), and color correct the entire movie.

The aesthetic challenge was making good on Frank Miller's vision and the groundwork laid in Albuquerque. "The 'Yellow Bastard' story we did in *Sin City* was good reference, but the big difference here was the Will Eisner factor, a lot of his signature things," St. John noted. "For example, violence doesn't take place up front and center, but in the shadows, or as silhouettes against a brick wall. And we weren't whacking people over the head with complex 3-D geometry. This was stylized 2-D graphical storytelling."

The supervisory work included providing vendors with "concept frames" representing stills from principle photography, with rough painted backgrounds as a guide for the photographic texture and "minimalism" Miller wanted. "It was a constant challenge to get these concept frames flowing so the vendors had something to start with, and also keep up with the Central City production," said visual effects supervisor Rich McBride. "*The Spirit* had to have some connection to the photographic world, which made it interesting working with the concept artists. Most artists in the movie business I've worked with are coming from a reality-based background, where everything needs to look photo-real, and they want to put in tons of detail to tell a story. To get artists to simplify and be selective about the types of detail was a bigger leap than I realized."

The Bunker itself was a small space. Through the main door, a cubbyhole of a reception area decorated with framed Eisner *Spirit* art opened into a central space with seven rooms housing everything from an Orphanage office (the effects house was officially treated as a separate vendor), to an editing suite, and the "DI suite," where real-time color correction was done with a Nucoda Film Master and interactive editorial meetings were held with visual effects vendors. Adjacent to the DI suite was the "War Room," where everything coming in and out was coordinated. Nancy St. John's team included line producer Kim Doyle, junior digital production manager Jaime Norman, junior visual effects

coordinator Danny Huerta, and digital production manager Paul Kolsanoff. Kolsanoff, along with lead compositor Bob Snyder, had been on set during filming to build a database of notes for camera angles, lenses, focal length, and other information for every shot that would be passed on to specific vendors.

To handle over 1,900 shots, St. John and Deborah Del Prete worked out a systematic process and schedule. All the shots in the movie were divided into sequences of twelve groups, which formed a system of "turnovers" that Del Prete and Miller would approve and turn over to Central City as official works-in-progress. The system included an overall budget which St. John and Kolsanoff prepared throughout principal photography for the services of the various effects companies. The turnover schedule was "a living document," St. John explained, that changed as editing came together, but always targeted hundreds of shots per turnover. "We had

Based in their Central City bunker in San Francisco's former military base, The Orphanage orchestrated the transformation of neutral greenscreen backgrounds into the illusion of a teeming city.

Above: A strolling Spirit gives a few words to a Central City reporter (Meeghan Holaway).

Above: A
silhouetted Frank
Miller and Deborah
Del Prete review
footage in the
Bunker.

Opposite:
Greenscreen
backgrounds
replaced with a
city environment
for a scene the
production dubbed
"Walk and Talk."

"The EDL references the HD Cam SR [high-definition camera, superior resolution] tapes we already have," Landau explained. "'Ingest' means we use that list to capture the high-resolution frames from the HD tapes and generate a low-res, QuickTime [QT] movie. We can then check and make sure everything is in synch. I can overlay the capture from our HD tapes. That movie I'm [then] putting over a cut-reference, that also comes from Odd Lot, and toggle between the two to see if there are any discrepancies, making sure everything is lining up, frame by frame. We're trying to match how they cut the film, and then we give that line-up information to the vendors. We then output a big EDL for a whole sequence into the Nucoda system here."

At his glowing monitors, Landau pulled up a QuickTime movie with a cut from Odd Lot showing the opening scene in the Spirit's inner sanctum. The Spirit walked across the stone floor, past his cats and silhouetted bars of the moonlit skylight. The scene was composed of thirteen separately shot plates, composited together. As if stripping layers away to an alternate reality, Landau toggled to footage prior to the official cut showing a cat trainer coming into frame to get a cat to stay in place. It would have been practically impossible, Landau noted, to get all the cats in place and acting properly at one time, so each element had to be shot separately and composited together.

Ultimately, the Bunker sent their effects houses a FireWire drive with all the data the vendors could download to process their shots — a QuickTime movie of the raw greenscreen cut, the QT with a Look Up Table applied, the original greenscreen plates, and the database information collected on set.

In the darkened DI suite, Stu Maschwitz was into the next step after a sequence had gone out — conferring with vendors on the work in progress. The cineSync session (cineSync being the software for interactive editorial reviews) was what Maschwitz called "remote collaborative dailies."

to be a machine, otherwise it wouldn't work, we'd miss. It sounds militaristic, but we were in the perfect place for it — in a bunker no less, in a War Room that was Command Central! My father was in the Air Force, so that thinking is easy for me."

March 13, 2008 was a snapshot day for life in the Bunker's *Spirit* world. On that day, the Central City team was deep into processing turnover #9, with only three turnovers to go. They were basically on schedule and definitely on budget, by St. John's estimates. "The life of a shot," as Aaron Rhodes put it, began with the locked-down cut sent from Odd Lot editorial, digital information that arrived as an EDL, for "Edit Decision List," a series of numbers for the greenscreen elements (or "plates") listing the beginning and end frames for each shot. Central City's lead editor, Ivan Landau, working with his assistants Anthony Reyna and David Fine, could then "ingest" that EDL information into their system.

Maschwitz, using his wireless Waycom tablet to draw directly on the footage, and with a speakerphone to converse with a client, sat in front of what was a mini-theater, with a screen and digital projector. Behind the screen was an enlargement of a Frank Miller storyboard of the Spirit rising from the Mudflats, with a message in red marker from Miller: "For The Orphanage — Charge ahead, you're in front of the pack!"

Maschwitz was in conference with Peter Lloyd, a concept artist in Oregon who would become an important contributor throughout post-production. They were discussing "Walk and Talk," a sequence where the Spirit, Commissioner Dolan, and trim, attractive young rookie officer Morgenstern briskly walk a roughly four-block section of Central City to the Donenfeld Building. On the screen, the greenscreen set backings had been color corrected to a more neutral gray. Set pieces indicated sidewalks or marked buildings and throughout audio of the actors played while extras enlivened the sequence, from passing pedestrians to construction workers. But other than the spectacular revolving door entrance of the Donenfeld Building, an entire urban environment needed to be conjured, including exteriors and interiors of the skyscraper itself.

As the sequence played, Maschwitz explained to Lloyd the area was analogous to midtown Manhattan, but without the glass and steel. As he talked, Maschwitz occasionally drew rough outlines of possible backgrounds on his tablet, which appeared in real time for both supervisor and client to see on their respective screens. At a post indicating the corner of what would become a CG building, the Spirit was met by a group of young autograph seekers, he signed a few

autographs, and was off with a cheery, "Play it straight, youngsters!" The walk passed what Maschwitz announced was "a Park Avenue kind of street," and he was back on the tablet, sketching a potential background as he noted the need for atmospheric haze. On screen, the flustered Dolan remonstrated with the masked crimefighter about his Octopus obsession. "He's up to something *big*," the Spirit responded.

Maschwitz noted the progression from a neighborhood area to a side street under construction, a narrow alley, and on to a grand boulevard and major business center, all of which had to be conjured out of the expanses of greenscreen cloaking the soundstage set. As the actors passed what was imagined as an alleyway, Maschwitz put pen to tablet and blacked the actors out. "You will get no flack from Frank [putting them in shadow]," he told Lloyd over speakerphone.

The sequence was designed to impart a sense of Central City as a real place, that the Spirit was hip to its shortcuts and navigating around town. "They go down this bigger business street," Maschwitz continued, "to a big, brass, gleaming Art Deco building. In a world full of other megalithic structures, [the Donenfeld Building] stands apart, it should be something cool."

As the actors on screen reached the revolving door, the effects supervisor mused about visual possibilities for the sweeping open space around the skyscraper. He wanted to avoid "Death Star trench," a reference to the battle-station trench in *Star Wars* that seemed to stretch to infinity, and asked Lloyd to block any to-infinity views with a building. Inside the skyscraper, Maschwitz requested a lavish lobby as impressive as the Empire State Building lobby, perhaps with

Above: Shot of the physical revolving door set piece with the greenscreen replaced by a digital building. See page 184 for the 'before' shot.

a mosaic inlaid floor. The supervisor and concept artist discussed the potential of lobby windows for providing light sources and dramatic shafts of light.

On screen, the masked man and officers entered an old elevator with a wrought iron cage that would be a black and white silhouette. "We're moving with them," Maschwitz said, as the elevator rose into "a graphical world" of silhouetted stairwells and rats scurrying up pipes. "Frank is known for his silhouettes, this is a nod to that," Maschwitz explained. In the end, ninety percent of the color would be sucked out, Maschwitz noted, with the exception of the Spirit's red tie. "There's a sepia, warm/gray overlook look, with hints of the natural hues of things," he added.

Later, after Stu Maschwitz had time to "decompress" following another cineSync session with Furious FX, he returned to the dark room for a DI color session. Maschwitz later noted he was actually working on a Nucoda Film Master and Digital Intermediate was the end result, but in the malleable way words and meanings evolve, the term "DI" had come to represent the process itself.

In any language, the digital color correction system allowed incredible freedom in manipulating color, a process that began even before Miller and Del Prete were scheduled to visit The Orphanage to review final shots. "We can make each frame like a Frank Miller painting," said Aaron Rhodes, who led the color work.

Color had always been important in movies, from the days of hand-tinted frames to three-strip Technicolor. But *Pleasantville* (1998) began taking color correction into the digital realm, while directors Joel and Ethan Coen, DP Roger Deakins, and Cinesite embraced the Digital Intermediate process in 2000 for *O Brother, Where Art Thou?* The system allowed filmmakers to balance and select color, from vast expanses to a gleam of light. "The DI basically gives us the ability to reconceive the film as it was shot into a completely different film," explained Rhodes. "While shooting, we had

the benefit of the LUTs, an approximation of what the final film would look like. I basically take those on-set instructions and implement them on a shot-by-shot basis with care and control. The DI process not only balances color from shot to shot, scene to scene, it can make a film feel cool or warm, good or horrific. You have enormous control. You can select a range of colors on a grand scale, isolate or combine them."

On the same screen used for viewing the cineSync sessions, Rhodes brought up an image of the Spirit tied up in the dentist's chair in the Octopus's lair. From behind a curtain, Plaster of Paris appeared as a deadly belly dancer, but a story point was she doesn't immediately recognize the Spirit, so the hero had to be in shadow. Before color correction, a close-up of Gabriel Macht's face looked warm, but as the color was drained away, his face went into shadow, except for an eerie brightness in his eyes. "As you under-expose him, there's detail in the bright highlights on his cheek, on the rope, there continues to be a lot of image there," Maschwitz noted. "The same thing if you went in the other direction and exposed up. There's a lot of information in the shadows. What that means is we have an incredibly robust and flexible image in terms of our ability to color correct. This is something that when Frank comes up, we're going to dial in interactively for this entire sequence. We're trying to keep these creative conversations alive throughout post-production. Darkening the Spirit's face is absolutely in the realm of an ordinary DI session, but what is not common is to be doing this simultaneously with the edit.

"In some ways, you could say we're re-lighting the scene, but this is *not* counter to the intention of the cinematographer," Maschwitz adds. "This is a conversation that started on set with

Opposite: The Spirit, a prisoner in the Octopus's lair, is confronted by the sultry Plaster of Paris and his nemesis in full Nazi regalia.

Above: In post-production, The Orphanage digitally manipulated colors, shadows, and densities — right down to the Spirit's bright eyes.

Above and
opposite: Plaster
of Paris has a
change of heart
and instead of
cutting the Spirit
up, cuts him
loose.

Frank, Bill Pope, and myself. Bill specifically lit this scene to not completely black out his face, knowing if he did we wouldn't be able to recover anything. But he placed shadows on the face in the right places so that in post we could enhance or adjust the shadows to make it work for Frank. In the DI you're not trying to undo or render obsolete decisions that were made on the set — you want to enhance those decisions. In this movie, the DI is happening simultaneously with the film coming together in visual effects, the color correction is not separate from the visual effects conversation. Usually, a director is doing color correction at the very end of the process and running through entire reels of film in a limited amount of time. With this film, we can sculpt over time."

Early in post-production, F.J. DeSanto along with all the other producers received a souvenir from The Orphanage, a framed picture of the first completed shot, a rooftop scene of a silhouetted Spirit in full sprint, his tie popping out in vibrant red. The shots to come would capture the look of a Frank Miller graphic novel.

Working in the digital realm it was possible to create something like "They Fight in Shadow," a shot of Spirit and Octopus battling as their shadows loomed dramatically in iconic comic book style. "I don't think ten years ago you could have done a shot like that and have people understand it," DeSanto reflected. "My first five years with Michael Uslan, he was trying to explain to people in our business that comic books were an acceptable source material. After *Spider-Man* and *X-Men*, it was about convincing people comics were more than just superheroes. Then came the graphic novel adaptations, like *Road to Perdition*. Now, with movies like *Sin City* and *300*, we're at the really cool point — literal adaptations of comic books. People are starting to understand them, and the technology has caught up with the imagination. Technology allows someone like Frank, who would normally draw this sort of thing, to successfully pull it off on the screen. What Eisner was trying to do fifty to sixty years ago was a cinematic take on comic books. Frank is just reversing that, bringing comic books to cinema."

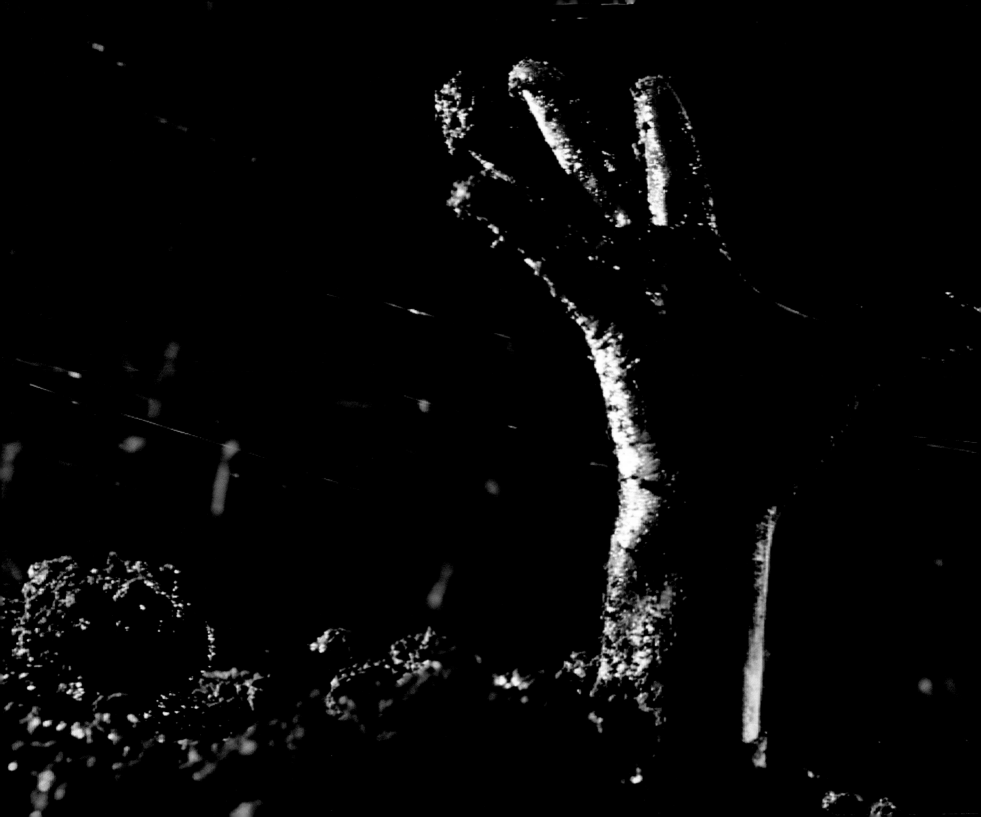

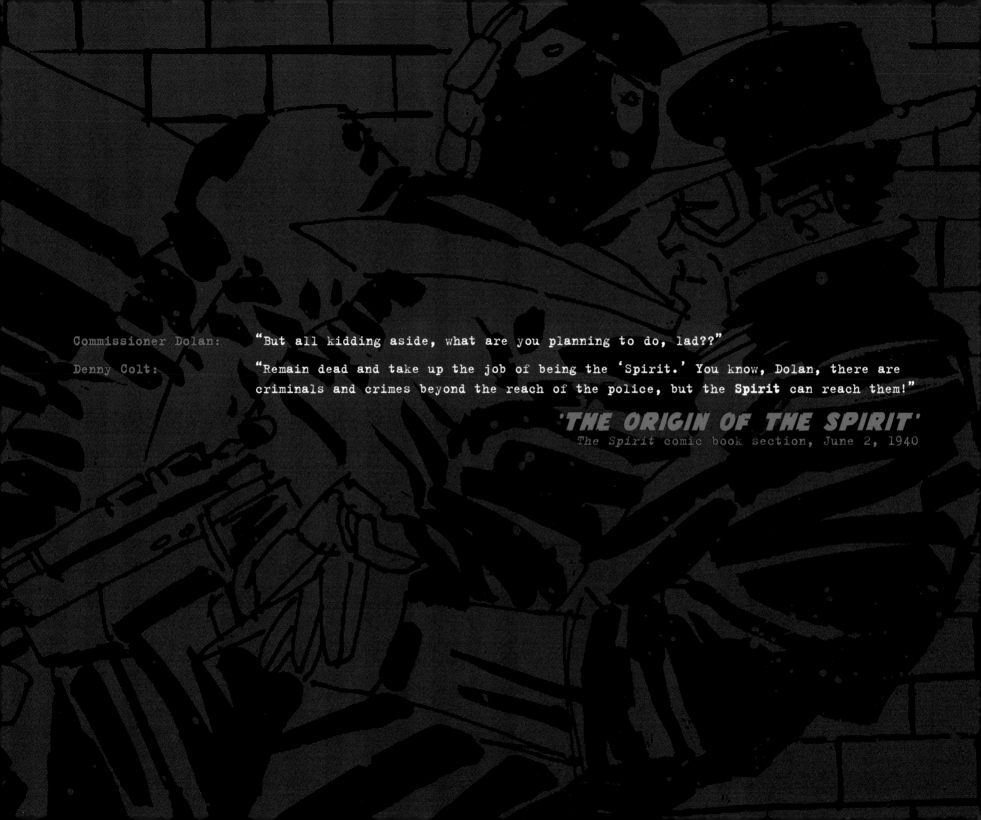

Commissioner Dolan: "But all kidding aside, what are you planning to do, lad??"

Denny Colt: "Remain dead and take up the job of being the 'Spirit.' You know, Dolan, there are criminals and crimes beyond the reach of the police, but the **Spirit** can reach them!"

'THE ORIGIN OF THE SPIRIT'
The *Spirit* comic book section, June 2, 1940

eath always shadowed the Spirit. In his origin tale, detective Denny Colt, eager for reward money, tries to single-handedly capture a master criminal known as Cobra, following narrow alleyways into the heart of Central City's Chinatown and descending into the Cobra's subterranean lab. In the ensuing battle, Colt is knocked out and drenched with a mysterious chemical that puts him in a state of suspended animation. The police discover Colt and, assuming he's dead, bury him in Wildwood Cemetery. Colt awakens and has to break out of his grave. Back on the trail of Cobra, he corners two crooks to learn the villain's whereabouts and announces, "I am the Spirit of good... but I can also be the Spirit of evil." By the time Cobra is captured, Commissioner Dolan knows the secret identity of the Spirit, the "dead" detective who was reborn as Central City's great crimefighter.

A grim origin, yet the series never made good on the psychological underpinning of a character whose path to crimefighting begins with a scenario out of Poe, a man buried alive and desperately clawing out of his grave. The Spirit wasn't alone among early comics heroes in surviving a traumatic event at the heart of his origin. A boy named Bruce Wayne saw his parents murdered, but for most of his Batman career was a grinning, almost carefree crimefighter. It would be a new generation of creators, notably the *Batman* team of artist Neal Adams and writer Denny O'Neil, who began drawing on the inherent darkness of the character.

But it was Frank Miller's four-part *Dark Knight* series that helped change perceptions of not only Batman, but the entire superhero genre, inspiring comics creators and filmmakers to go behind the masks of the vaunted superheroes and face their psychological depths, even deconstruct the superhero myth and ponder what the world would really be like with superheroes in it. When asked if he brought out the dramatic dimensions of the Spirit's horrific resurrection, Miller said quietly: "I think I did."

F.J. DeSanto, involved in the early story development process, recalls the movie initially wasn't going to touch on the Spirit's origin. "But as the script progressed, we needed to understand what happened to this guy — he's living on borrowed time! What I think was key for Frank was he's a guy protecting his city, so when you see him clawing out of that grave he's not just trying to save himself — he knows he has to do more!"

Denny Colt's "buried alive moment" was played out in a color palette of black and white and red, with the interior of

Above: The "death" of
Denny Colt.

Colt's coffin backlit and illuminated in bright white light, "sort of the way Frank would draw it," Maschwitz explained. "There's a good strain of visual symbolism in this movie, and probably the biggest 'aha' moment for Frank, Bill, and me collectively was the flashback sequence where we get a little bit of the origin story of Denny Colt. It's not uncommon to have the color red associated with death in a movie, but we have a movie that's almost purely black and white. So we played the flashback scenes with vivid reds, and the tie is like an affectation he carries around with him to remind him of what he is, to remind him that he did die. He was Denny Colt, a cop who's killed and somehow manages to come back from the dead and become the Spirit. The fact that he's dead is the thing that makes him a superhero and what makes him look like a superhero is this bright red tie — the red tie is like his Superman cape."

A .45 COLT TYPE PISTOL

I AM A **GUN**
AN INSTRUMENT OF DEATH...
A MURDER WEAPON
HARDENED...
IN THE FIRES OF HATE...
CONCEIVED WITH COLD
CUNNING OF A KILLER'S
MIND......
"**DEATH IS MY DESTINY**

BY Will Eisner

Left: Eisner dealt with the subject of death in many ways. This 1951 story is told from the gun's perspective.

Next spread: A vision of the women in the Spirit's life, from storyboard to final frame.

SPIRIT
DRIFTS
ABOVE FACES
-
HIS SHADOW
CRAWLS
ACROSS
THEM
-
THINK
MOUNT
RUSH
MORE
-

I SEE
SWEET
ELLEN,
ALWAYS
PUTTING
MY
RAGGED
PIECES
BACK
TOGETHER
...

...THORNE,
POWDER
PUFF...

It was a cool and sunny day in San Francisco, the last week of March 2008, when Frank Miller, dressed in a black fedora and a black *300* T-shirt emblazoned on the back with "Tonight we dine in Hell," met Deborah Del Prete at the Hyatt Regency, a hotel that rises above the California Street cable car tracks and overlooks the waterfront ferry building. It was late morning and a car was set to whisk them across town to the Presidio and their first visit to the Central City Bunker and the first DI color correction review session.

The director and producer talked about the movie and got to the strange case of the Spirit's origin. They had been determined not to do a typical origin story, but their hero was too rooted in Wildwood Cemetery and the macabre goings-on

I LOVE YOU SO.

ENTER ME.

ENTER ME AND NEVER LEAVE ME AGAIN.

connected with the rumored death and burial of detective Denny Colt. At the end of the day, Del Prete said, they have a flashback origin story.

Miller noted the Spirit's origin was about transformation and what he called "his dance with death," which took the form of Jaime King's Lorelei, the siren who seems to call the Spirit back to the grave. "Death is always nearby, and death as played by Jaime King is really appealing," Miller said. "It gives an erotic edge to his endless dance with death. But it's Lincoln's quote about having greatness thrust upon you. Denny Colt had a life that made sense. He was going to college to be a cop, he was going to marry Ellen Dolan, maybe even be police commissioner someday, who knows? But he was murdered… and buried. And now he's something else. That's what this movie is about."

Deborah Del Prete added that Denny Colt was on a search to explore the riddle of his existence. "It's the ultimate existential crisis — who am I, what am I doing here, why am I alive? Nobody really knows that anyway, but what I love about the movies is any time you give a voice to what's essentially people's ultimate fears and questions about life, that's very relatable and understandable. For me, it's always about that one person alone in the dark [of the movie theater]. That's an incredibly powerful thing we do, to say, 'I get that, I'm scared of dying too.' Because, in a way, that's what this movie is about."

Previous spread (left): Lorelei. Jaime King, a *Sin City* veteran, shares a laugh with the director.

Previous spread (right): Miller storyboard art, Lorelei prepares to give the Spirit the kiss of death.

Left, and opposite: Shooting Lorelei and Spirit on the greenscreen stage, and final frames from the sequence.

John Medlen recalls he was in heaven when he got to be stunt fight coordinator on the first *Spider-Man* movie, helping bring to life one of the great comic book heroes. On *The Spirit*, he was back in that wonderful world of pure fantasy. "I guess we always have the little kid in us somewhere, and in the movie industry that's where we get to pretend and play and get paid for it. To create something and let the audience enjoy the new technologies of CG and effects which brings these old comic books to life — it's great! What more could you ask for?"

"The comic book explosion fosters the development and advancement of CGI — that's all to the good!" Ben Melniker noted. "It's incredible to think you could have had a motion picture industry that was so successful without the enhancement brought about by comic book movies. It shows how flexible the motion picture world is that it could shift the way it has."

For some, like Michael Dennison, the new technology prompted soul-searching questions. "*The Spirit* immersed me in this new technology of filmmaking, this greenscreen process and all the work that can go on after the fact. I was mesmerized by it, but at the same time, I thought, 'Hmmm, I wonder if there's going to be a costume designer in ten years?!' Maybe things will evolve where the costume designer will build a textural black and white or neutral costume and they'll morph it into anything they want. I hope our industry remains true to the human touch, that it's a brain, talent, and Muse process that I don't think is duplicated technologically. But they can now change the color of everything, they can make it snow in the middle of a movie! You design something in black because it's part of the character and somewhere down the line, they can make it pink because they think it's better. This experience was kind of a springboard to those thoughts."

"Will Eisner was a treasure shared by three tribes.

"Will was a gem for the people of New York City....

"Will was true gold for the immigrant Jews who journeyed to America, and their children. Not the false dreamer's gold that the streets were supposedly paved with, but the pure glittering metal of the artist's pen that captured a moment in time forever, etching it indelibly so that we could return to the Lower East Side as it was when our families came here....

"And Will was a natural resource so great as to be a landmark for the people of comics."

PAUL LEVITZ[1]

"The comic strip is no longer a comic strip but in reality an illustrated novel. It is new and raw just now, but material for a limitless, intelligent development. And eventually, and inevitably, it will be a legitimate medium for the best of writers and artists."

WILL EISNER, 1942[2]

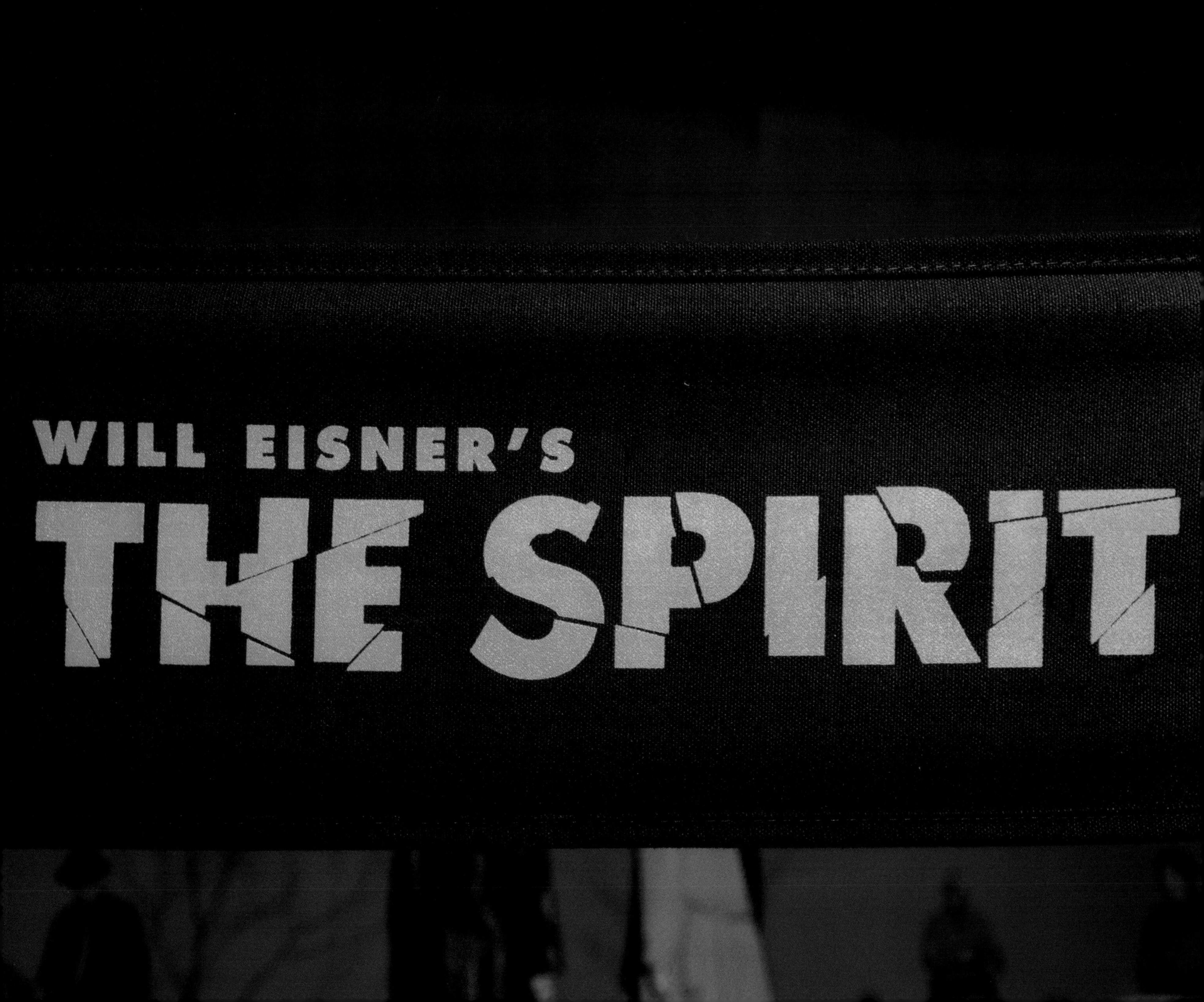
WILL EISNER'S
THE SPIRIT

On a peninsula called Strawberry Point sits a house on a hill with a deck like the bow of a ship, with a curved railing allowing one to lean into spectacular views of San Francisco Bay. A small glass pyramid on the deck forms a skylight for a studio below full of Native American art, one of publisher Malcolm Whyte's artistic interests. A collector of original comics art, in 1984 he founded the Cartoon Art Museum in San Francisco, a nonprofit museum dedicated to the then fantastic proposition that comics were a legitimate art form. He met Will Eisner in the early 1980s, and the artist became one of the fledgling museum's professional advisors.

Sitting in his living room, sunshine streaming through the picture window bay views, Whyte pulled out original art for a seven-page Eisner story, lavishly drawn and inked on twenty-two inch long by fifteen-inch wide illustration board. 'Blood of the Earth', first published in February 26, 1950, was a retelling of the Spirit's exotic adventure in Damascus, that tale Jules Feiffer famously included in *The Great Comic Book Heroes*. As in the earlier tale, the Spirit journeys to the Middle East and finds Dr. Gregg, bitter and

dissolute expatriate from Central City, in the backroom of a shadowy saloon. Once again, a jewel worn by Sheikh Ali Bey's daughter figures in the action, but rather than a jewel of death it's a "stone of immortality," the Jewel of Gizeh. The Sheikh controls land sitting upon a sea of oil, but it's said he will sell his oil land to the one who finds his lost daughter, kidnapped fifty years ago. The Spirit knows men will kill for that black gold, and believes Gregg knows the whereabouts of the jewel and the lost daughter. Sand Saref is also in on the chase, her sultry eyes dazzled by the allure of the immortal jewel. In the end, father and daughter are reunited, Gregg is revealed as the daughter's husband and heir to the oil land (the riches of which he promises to use to rebuild the kingdom), and Gregg hands the jewel to the Spirit to take to the Central City Museum. Sand begs Spirit to reconsider his idealistic crimefighting notions: "Team up with me, we'll knock them all dead." The Spirit refuses. "You dumb starry-eyed idiot," she groans as they kiss. They part and the Spirit, looking over his shoulder, tells Sand the jewel she *just lifted* is phony: "I've got the real Jewel of Gizeh safely tucked to my starry-eyed, idealistic heart!!"[3]

Above: *Spirit*
promotion rolls
out with bus and
train advertising.

Opposite: Sarah
Paulson and Eva
Mendes, Tim Palen
Spirit promotional
photography.

Next spread:
Spirit promotional
posters.

Whyte held up the first splash page and noted the archway under which sat the familiar old soothsayer who, as in the original story, has traced the face of the Spirit in the sand. The soothsayer is next seen in the final panel, sitting in the shadows of the archway as a flummoxed Sand stands arms akimbo and the Spirit, framed in dark silhouette, waves farewell. "'Blood of the Earth' opens as the 'curtain rises' on an Arabesque style gateway, and goes into this exotic story of mystery, adventure, and romance," Whyte noted. "At the end, the curtain comes down and fades to black on the Arabesque cut-out the story opened with. To me, this refers to all the theatrical strings pulling on him. Will's father was a theatrical scene painter, and Will got into the act. Will grew up in a tough part of town, with immigrants who all brought their stories. He grew up with the early movies, the non-talkies which were all black and white, and the pulps, which had blood and thunder stories and were illustrated on scratchboard for dramatic chiaroscuro effects. All of these things were shaping him. He knew how to do bird's eye or worm's eye views and silhouettes — all the tricks of the camera. He made movies on paper!"

Whyte pointed to a moon-shaped Indian mask hanging on the wall of his living room entranceway. "The first time I met Will, I invited him and a few people to come over to the house. Will came in and saw that mask. It's a painted Hawkman in the Moon cedar mask, a power symbol from the Northwest Coast Indians, and has blue paint, like a mask, around the eyes. Will whirled around, pointed up at it, and said, 'Copyright infringement!' I was pouring wine, and Will and my friend Larry Evans went out on the deck and were enjoying this view. Will came back in and said, 'You know, my father was a scene painter, and Larry and I had a great idea that some night we'd sneak up here with a big canvas and paint a bunch of tenements on it and hang it behind these windows, so when you look out in the morning you'll see this dreary tenement scene.' So, there he was — back in the theatrical world. That was the first time I met him. Will was a true and honest gentleman of the Old School."

In Frank Miller's *Spirit* script, the crimefighter takes time to survey the city he loves and protects. "My city," he thinks, "an old city… She doesn't hide what she is. What she's made of. The sweat and muscle and blood of generations."

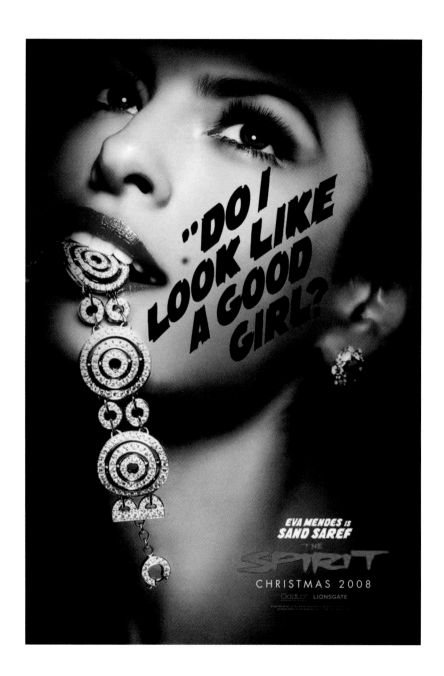

```
Will Eisner's The Spirit

a screenplay by

Frank Miller




Based on the comic series created by Will Eisner




                              2ND PINK REVISIONS 11/1/07
                              2ND BLUE REVISIONS 10/30/07
                              2ND WHITE REVISIONS 10/29/07
                                 BUFF REVISIONS 10/23/07
                               SALMON REVISIONS 10/8/07
                                ALL GOLDENROD 10/2/07
                                  ALL GREEN 9/27/07
                                 ALL YELLOW 9/25/07
                                   ALL PINK 9/17/07
                                   ALL BLUE 9/11/07
                      2nd White Production Draft 8/8/07
```

Right: The bible of the production, the Frank Miller screenplay with final revisions (11/1/'07).

Opposite: "My City Screams," a Spirit phrase from the script, became the signature tagline during the film's promotional campaign.

Following Miller's delineation of the real Central City — the section of Manhattan bounded by Houston and Jane — one can follow Houston eastward to the border of the Lower East Side, the district whose immigrant spirit and Jewish culture flourished when Eisner created *The Spirit*. "The Jewish culture has always been one of hand-me-down oral traditions and storytelling," Michael Uslan reflected. "Will was so influenced by Yiddish theater and many of the things that took place in lower New York."

The Lower East Side has changed mightily since Eisner's early days. Addresses where Yiddish theaters once thrived no longer even exist, or have been replaced by modern structures of glass and steel. The synagogue where the Will Eisner memorial service was held reflected the post-war changes. The synagogue having been built in 1849 as an architectural marvel inspired by the Cathedral of Cologne, it had been abandoned by the 1980s, when Spanish artist Angel Orensanz purchased the sacred relic and gave it new life as an arts and community center.[4]

A few landmarks of Will Eisner's personal history still stand. From the Lower East Side, heading south in lower Manhattan, is one address: 37 Wall Street. It was in front of this ornate old building that Eisner stood as a newsboy hawking newspapers, a time when the wonderful comics page took hold of him and didn't let go. After World War II, he became a tenant here, moving his studio and continuing his work on *The Spirit*.[5] Other than venerable Trinity Church down the street, Will was surrounded by seats and citadels of political and economic power: Federal Hall, where George Washington took the oath of office as first U.S. President; the stock exchange; corporate headquarters. For a son of immigrants, Wall Street had to represent the epitome of success, particularly when the boy became a young adult with dreams of getting people to take comics seriously.

Eisner's studio on Wall Street was a far cry from the old studio he had uptown at 5 Tudor City, where the Spirit was born. Many times, Eisner must have passed the *New York Daily News* building on 42nd Street on his way up the hill where, once upon a time, goats grazed and squatters squatted but which was then a development imagined in the 1920s as an urban oasis in a slum area. When Eisner created the Spirit, hilltop Tudor City overlooked the slaughterhouses on the East River. That grim stretch of Blood Alley has long since been swept away, replaced by the United Nations building, but it's not hard to imagine Eisner taking a break from *The Spirit* and gazing out in wind and all kinds of weather to the East River and the colorful sights, and smells, of Blood Alley. It was a different time, when Eisner brought the Spirit to life. The year his masked crimefighter was born, Denmark, Norway, Belgium, and France had already fallen under the Nazi juggernaut and America's entrance into the world war was still more than a year away.

For those who worked on the movie, getting to know Eisner and his character became about more than just connecting with the glamour of a bygone era. "He came from a real rough, intense world, the time of World War II," set decorator Gabrielle Petrissans reflected. "I didn't know Will Eisner before this show, but I read a lot about him. He didn't come from any kind of privilege. His way of coming to terms with a very rough world was he invented heroes and amazingly strong women. His drawings helped him find some kind of hope in that darkness."

Eisner had drawn from the world around him to fashion his *Spirit* world, and the Miller movie had drawn upon that to build a contemporary recreation of the Spirit and Central City. "Frank would pull everybody back and say, 'That scene needs a water tower in the background, that would be very Will Eisner,'" Nancy St. John recalled. "This film is really Frank's tribute to Will Eisner and his Spirit."

"Not a day went by on that set when Frank didn't ask, 'Am I doing Will justice?'" Gigi Pritzker noted. "Sometimes he voiced it, but most of the time it was clear. That was of critical importance to him."

By April of 2008, *The Spirit* promotional machine was gearing up. The movie was a presence at the New York Comic Con, where the first *Spirit* trailer was unveiled on Saturday, April 19. A billboard campaign, emblazoned with the line from the script, "My City Screams," kicked off in New York and Los Angeles. By July, *The Spirit* was a major presence at the Comic-Con in San Diego, but unlike the last panel introducing Frank Miller as the writer/director, there was now a film to talk about.

This page: Frank Miller as Officer Liebowitz of the Central City police department. Miller also made a cameo in *Sin City* as a corrupt priest who meets a violent end in his confessional.

For many production principals, there were poignant memories of Comic-Con 2004, the one that was Eisner's last. Deborah Del Prete remembers walking around the floor with Will, as he marveled at how the convention had become a huge promotional machine for movies born by himself and, as he put it, "a few other guys in these little rooms in New York City" all those years ago.

From option agreement to finished film had taken around fifteen years — in all his years at MGM, Ben Melniker noted, he had never seen an option take so long to reach fruition. But, at the end of the day, the final result had been worth the wait. And all the production principals agreed that making *The Spirit* was *fun*, that there had been an infectious, creative joy working with Miller, and creative freedom bringing a comic book world to life.

"I'm now a convert [to comics]," laughed producer Gigi Pritzker. "For us at Odd Lot, *The Spirit* is a huge step in our learning curve and our tool box. Both Deb and I would love to work with Frank again, and in a variety of ways, not just comics. Frank opened our eyes to potential things and ways we can do things."

"When you make movies the way we do, which is passionately, it's not about the outside stuff," Del Prete said, dismissing the perceived "glamour" of the business. "My husband and I recently celebrated our twenty-fifth wedding anniversary and Frank was there and I made a little speech stating that I don't make movies, I birth them. But it *is* that. You get to bond with people in an extraordinary way, you get to know each other in ways you wouldn't have anticipated as you work on something that will be seen by millions of people. Frank and I got to do this journey together."

"In the end, I don't think we did *Sin City* squared, to be honest," Bill Pope reflected. "There's still a lot of naturalism in this movie. But that's relative. It was going to be super-stylized no matter what. It wasn't just our vanity that wanted to do *Sin City* squared — that's where Frank's script and his direction

told us to go. That inspired us and gave us license to push it as far as we could. But is it more stylized than *Sin City*? I don't think so."

To Pope, one of the pleasures of the production had been working with Miller. Whatever concerns there might have been about his solo directorial debut, Pope always felt they were in sure hands. "What happened on *Sin City* I can only guess, but he had his trial by fire. He was already fully grown on this one. He's a one-of-a-kind artist, a genius. He does something no one else does or could do, and it just springs out of him — a look, a feeling, a mood. It was a genuine pleasure to watch him [direct]."

"It is a journey and there are so many twists and turns because it's such a big ship you're trying to captain when making a movie," Miller concluded. "I never had this much responsibility and authority before. I learned every damn day on the set and it was an exhilarating and exhausting experience. I've come out of it a different person, with a different set of skills. I'll never look at movies the same way again."

The only thing missing was Will Eisner himself. "It's sad for me that he's not going to be here to see the release of this film," Uslan said. "But what's important to me is that on that day I can go up to [Will's wife] Ann and say, 'I delivered on what I promised your husband.'"

The Spirit died in 1952 but endured, not unlike Denny Colt himself, kept alive in reprint collections. But the creator himself avoided resurrecting the Spirit for a fresh run of stories. Publisher Denis Kitchen, whose Kitchen Sink publishing house reprinted classic *Spirit* stories, was one of many who kept after Eisner about returning to his most famous character. "The fan in me was curious," Kitchen once said. "*The Spirit* dropped off in 1952. It didn't end as gracefully as people who loved it hoped it would... I said [to Eisner], 'How about one last hurrah?' He always resisted it."[6]

Eisner had moved on, pursuing his vision of comics as "sequential art" (and wrote a book on the subject, *Comics and Sequential Art*), and pioneered the graphic novel. He influenced a generation of comics creators, and was a rich resource for *The Amazing Adventures of Kavalier & Clay*, Michael Chabon's Pulitzer Prize-winning novel of the Golden Age of Comics. His very name became the gold standard for the best in comics with the establishment in 1987, under the auspices of the San Diego Comic-Con, of the annual Will Eisner Comics Industry Awards.

In the last month of Eisner's life, he completed what he felt was his most powerful work: *The Plot: The Secret History of* The Protocols of the Elders of Zion. In a preface, written the month before he died, Eisner announced the work was "a

departure from pure graphic story-telling." *The Protocols*, first published in Russia in 1905, purported to reveal a Jewish plot for world domination but was, in reality, an anti-Semitic tract whose claims and authenticity were long ago debunked and exposed by scholars and historians. But still it lived — *lives today* — and Eisner felt the emergence of graphic novels as popular literature could expose the lie to a wider audience and "drive yet another nail into the coffin of this terrifying vampire-like fraud."[7]

The Plot was a fitting final graphic novel, but it wasn't the end. There was one final Eisner work-in-progress to be published — the last *Spirit* story.

The day before he went in for his fateful hospital visit,

SAND GRABS
BOXES BY
STRAP

Eisner delivered a six-page *Spirit* story to Dark Horse Comics editor Diana Schutz. It posthumously appeared in *The Amazing Adventures of the Escapist*, the comic book series based on the fictional Golden Age escape artist superhero Michael Chabon created in *Kavalier & Clay*. "Will Eisner did *not* want to do this story," Schutz opened in an introductory essay under the words: "WILL EISNER March 6, 1917–January 3, 2005." Eisner had long ago left the character to pursue stories about real people in the real world, not "the pursuit-and-vengeance" genre conventions of comic book heroes, she noted. But she kept asking and, finally, Eisner said he'd do a Spirit story, and when he made a promise he always came through. "It is both fitting and ironic that this should be Will's last work," she wrote, "…that Will should come full circle and leave us with this one last Spirit story…."[8]

In the story, the Spirit is captured by thugs sent by his old flame, P'Gell. He is trussed up, imprisoned in a brick cell, taunted by the femme fatale (looking heavier, but no less amorous since her prime). The Spirit discovers he is not alone — P'Gell has captured the Escapist and is asking a heavy ransom from Chabon to get him back. Together, the masked heroes help each other escape. "I was saved by a superhero," Spirit smiles. "Wow, Eisner will have an ulcer if he ever hears about it!"

"Tell me, Escapist," Spirit asks, as they race across the rooftops to freedom, "have you ever wondered what heroes do for society?"

"Don't have much time to dwell on 'why,'" the Escapist muses, "but I guess what we give are instant solutions and happy endings! Society just wants to watch us do it again and again! Eh, Spirit?"

The Spirit gives the Escapist the precious item a courier died for, the treasure P'Gell was after: a first edition of *Kavalier & Clay*. "Now, that is a happy ending!" the Escapist declares, as he and the Spirit stand silhouetted against a full moon.

It was a fitting salute from the old cartoonist to the young novelist. But, promises aside, why *did* Will Eisner create this last Spirit story? Perhaps he saw it as an ironic Eisner-esque story — the old cartoonist returning to his drawing board and the heroic character who sprang from the fertile imagination of his youth. Perhaps he was letting off steam, frustrated with the interminable wait for the *Spirit* movie. Perhaps his Spirit was calling to him like a long-lost old friend….

No matter. In the end, Will Eisner couldn't escape the Spirit. And maybe it's enough to know that, in his last days, he was dreaming of happy endings. Certainly, the story of *The Spirit* movie had a happy ending. The final motion picture was not a cold monument, like the vine-covered stone and marble memorials in the tangled, weedy overgrowth of abandoned Wildwood Cemetery. That was what Frank Miller wanted to avoid. In the end it was, as has been said, a tribute and its own unique thing.

The Spirit lives.

NOTES

Unless otherwise footnoted, all quotes are from exclusive interviews with the author. Quotes from actors Samuel Jackson, Eva Mendes, Scarlett Johansson, and Dan Lauria are from *The Spirit* electronic press kit interviews conducted by Eric Matthies Productions, Inc. (and edited for continuity).

Chapter One: The Shadow of The Spirit

1: James Steranko, *The Steranko History of Comics*, Volume 2 (Reading, Pennsylvania: Supergraphics, 1972), p. 116.

2: Jules Feiffer, *The Great Comic Book Heroes* (New York: The Dial Press, 1965), pp. 35–36.

3: 'The real beginning', essay by Tom Heintjes, *Spirit No. 1: The Origin Years*, Kitchen Sink Press, May 1992.

4: David Hajdu, *The Ten-Cent Plague: The Great Comic Book Scare and How it Changed America* (New York: Farrar, Straus and Giroux, 2008), p. 24.

5: Bob Andelman, *Will Eisner: A Spirited Life* (Milwaukie, OR: M Press, 2005), pp. 52–54; for details of Eisner & Iger passing on *Superman*, see page 43.

6: Steranko, *History of Comics*, Vol. 2, p. 116.

7: John Benson interview with Will Eisner, 'Having Something to Say', *The Comics Journal* #267 (April/May 2005), p. 116.

8: 'An introduction to the Wally Wood Spirits', essay by Will Eisner, *The Spirit* #20, Kitchen Sink Enterprises, 1979.

9: Hajdu, *The Ten-Cent Plague*, p. 228.

10: Charles Brownstein, interviewer, *Eisner/Miller* (Milwaukie, Oregon: Dark Horse Books, 2005), Introduction, p. 3.

11: 'Frank Miller The Interviews: 1981–2003', *The Comics Journal Library*, Fantagraphics Books, 2003, Interview one, p. 15.

Chapter Two: The Comic Book Movie

1: The 2008, 38th edition of the bible of comics collecting, the *Official Overstreet Comic Book Price Guide*, lists a near mint copy of that first Spider-Man story at $50,000. Uslan recalls that at a comics auction at the Broadway Central convention, *Action* #1, the first appearance of Superman, sold for $40 — today, *Overstreet* lists a near mint copy at $675,000. Uslan and Klein decided to bid on *Batman* #1 and pooled $22 between them, with Uslan's dad throwing an extra $5 into the pot. Their $27 dollar offer lost out to a $29 bid — *Overstreet* lists a near mint copy of that landmark book at $185,000.

2: Will Eisner obituary by Sarah Boxer of *The New York Times*, run in the *San Francisco Chronicle*, January 5, 2005; Eisner "eyewitness" comments from *A Contract with God* ad essay, *The Spirit* #18, Kitchen Sink Enterprises, 1978.

3: 'Writing the rules', article by Tom Heintjes, *Spirit No. 4: The Origin Years*, Kitchen Sink reprint, November 1992, p. 8.

4: Andelman, *Will Eisner*, pp. 54–55.

5: Brownstein, *Eisner/Miller*, pp. 137, 201.

6: 'Meet P'Gell' story, October 6, 1946; 'The Story of Gerhard Shnobble', September 5, 1948; 'Lorelei Rox', September 19, 1948; 'Ten Minutes', September 11, 1949. These classic tales are collected in *The Best of The Spirit*, DC Comics, 2005.

7: Mark Evanier tribute, *Comic Book Artist*, November 2005, p. 116.

Chapter Three: Never World

1: Frank Miller and Robert Rodriguez, *Frank Miller's Sin City: The Making of the Movie* (Troublemaker Publishing, 2005), pp. 127, 193.

2: Jody Duncan, 'Cool Cars, Hot Women and Hard Bastard Men', *Cinefex* #102, July 2005: pp. 29–30.

3: 'The Art of War', by Lev Grossman, *Time*, March 12, 2007: p. 58.

4: Mark Cotta Vaz and Craig Barron, *The Invisible Art: The Legends of Movie Matte Painting* (San Francisco: Chronicle Books, 2002), p. 57.

5: *Sin City* DVD two-disc "recut-extended-unrated" edition, feature commentary: Robert Rodriguez & Frank Miller; 5:01–5:07 mark.

6: Raymond Chandler, *The Simple Art of Murder* (New York: Ballantine Books, 1977), p. 20.

7: Miller and Rodriguez, *Sin City*, p. 11; crime comic reference from *Comics Journal Library*, Miller Interviews, p. 80.

8: Ibid., pp. 81, 91.

9: Ibid., p. 21.

Chapter Four: Cast of Characters

1: First quote from *The Spirit* Electronic Press Kit (EPK), Eric Matthies Productions, Inc. Additional EPK quotes from Mendes, Johansson, and Jackson.

Chapter Five: The Green World and Black World

1: Dan Lauria and Samuel Jackson, EPK quotes.

Chapter Eight: The Spirit Lives

1: Paul Levitz, president and publisher of DC Comics, from introductory essay to *Will Eisner: A Retrospective*, a 2005 Eisner exhibition catalogue published by the Museum of Comic and Cartoon Art of New York City.

2: Eisner quote, 'Blithe Spirit' article, *Comic Book Artist*, November 2005, p. 5.

3: Whyte inscribed, on the back of page 1 of this original art, that Jules Feiffer wrote this story, Andre LeBlanc provided background inks, and Abe Kenegser lettered.

4: Historical background from Angel Orensanz Foundation website.

5: Eisner address information for Wall Street and Tudor City from 'Editor's Note' by Denis Kitchen in *Will Eisner's New York: Life in the Big City* (New York: W.W. Norton & Company, 2006), p. xi.

6: Adelman, *Will Eisner*, p. 304.

7: Will Eisner preface, *The Plot: The Secret History of* The Protocols of the Elders of Zion (New York: W.W. Norton & Company, 2005), pp. 1, 3.

8: *The Amazing Adventures of The Escapist*, #6, Dark Horse Comics, April 2005.

My special thanks to Titan Books and editor Adam Newell for allowing me to make this trip to Central City. I'm particularly indebted to Frank Miller, Deborah Del Prete, Michael Uslan, and the whole company for supporting this work. Lionsgate came through big time in the personages of Aubrey McClure and Jacqueline Ghaemmaghami, who helped facilitate connections with the many interview subjects and supplied material vital for understanding and writing about this production. And thanks to the good folks down in "the Bunker," with special appreciation to Stu Maschwitz, Nancy St. John, and everyone at The Orphanage who took time to explain that thing we call "movie magic."

Thanks to the keepers of the Eisner flame, including publisher Denis Kitchen, whose *Spirit* reprints reached a new generation, and Carl and Nancy Gropper, who run Will Eisner Studios, Inc., and are faithful stewards of Eisner's work and legacy.

My deep appreciation, as always, to my agent John Silbersack of the Trident Media Group, and his assistant Libby Kellogg, for their efforts in booking passage for me into the *Spirit* world.

And a big tip of the Spirit's fedora to F.J. DeSanto, who made *Spirit* connections for me during a wonderful New York trip, and to my friend and colleague Steve Saffel, with whom I made an "Eisner Walk" one chilly and overcast day in Manhattan, visiting places of interest to Will Eisner's personal history that ranged from Tudor City to the Lower East Side and Wall Street.

As usual, my pal Bruce Walters did another excellent author's photo (and thanks to Nick Waller for the assist).

All my love to my family and my magnificent mother, who proof-read this manuscript. And here's a shout-out to my dear friend Brian Connolly, who was with me in spirit during the journey of this book — Brian! This one's for *you*, brother!

— M.C.V.

Titan Books would also like to thank Aubrey McClure, Jacqueline Ghaemmaghami, Tim Palen and Sarah Greenberg at Lionsgate, Al Newman at Odd Lot, and the entire cast and crew of *The Spirit*, with special appreciation to Frank Miller for his Introduction.

Mark Cotta Vaz is a *New York Times* bestselling author and this *Spirit* book is his twenty-fifth published work. His books include *Tales of the Dark Knight*, the authorized fiftieth anniversary history of the Batman character, and *The Invisible Art: The Legends of Movie Matte Painting* (co-authored with Academy of Motion Picture Arts and Sciences Board of Governors member Craig Barron), which won best-book awards from The Theatre Library Association (TLA) of New York and the United States Institute of Theatre Technology. Vaz's critically acclaimed biography, *Living Dangerously: The Adventures of Merian C. Cooper, Creator of* King Kong, made the *Los Angeles Times* bestseller list in 2005 and was a TLA finalist selection. Vaz is a past member of the board of directors of

Lionsgate and Odd Lot Entertainment Present
an Odd Lot Entertainment/Lionsgate Production

THE SPIRIT

Based on the comic book series created by Will Eisner

Written for the Screen and Directed by Frank Miller

Produced by	Deborah Del Prete Gigi Pritzker Michael E. Uslan
Executive Producers	Benjamin Melniker Steven Maier William Lischak
Executive Producers	Michael Burns Michael Paseornek
Co-Producers	Linda McDonough F.J. DeSanto
Co-Executive Producer	Jeff Andrick

CAST	(in order of appearance)
Lorelei	Jaime King
Spirit	Gabriel Macht
Detective Sussman	Dan Gerrity
Arthur The Cat	Himself
Damsel in Distress	Kimberly Cox
Thug 1	Brian Lucero
Thug 2	David B. Martin
Officer MacReady	Larry Reinhardt-Meyer
Liebowitz	Frank Miller
Sand Saref	Eva Mendes
Mahmoud	Eric Balfour
Octopus	Samuel L. Jackson
Pathos, etc.	Louis Lombardi
Silken Floss	Scarlett Johansson
Ellen	Sarah Paulson
Dolan	Dan Lauria
Medic	Dan Hubbert
Young Spirit	Johnny Simmons
Young Sand	Seychelle Gabriel
Uncle Pete	Michael Milhoan
Mafioso	John Cade
Officer Saref	David Wiegand
Reporter	Chad Brummett
Donenfeld	Richard Portnow
Seth	Mark DelGallo
Morgenstern	Stana Katic
Handbag Thief	Aaron Toney
Handbag Man	Dean Eldon Squibb
Female Reporter	Meeghan Holaway
Poker Player	Al Goto
Doorman #1	Roman Tissera
Doorman #2	Frank Bond
Doorman #3	Hugh Elliott
Onlooker #1	Robert Douglas Washington
Onlooker #2	Bill Pope
Son	Ben Petry
Young Mother	Marina Lyon
Onlooker #3	Paul Levitz
Onlooker #4	Emily Cheung
Onlooker #5	Keith K,hl
Onlooker #6	Cayley Bell
Onlooker #7	Jasmine Mohamed
Plaster of Paris	Paz Vega
Muffin	Sammy / Spirit / Stewie
Wino	T. Jay O'Brien
Creep	Rio Alexander
Officer Klink	Drew Pollock
Finger Puppeteer	Andy Linderkamp

CREW

Director of Photography	Bill Pope
Art Director	Rosario Provenza
Editor	Gregory Nussbaum
Costume Designer	Michael Dennison
Music by	David Newman
Senior Visual Effects Supervisor	Stu Maschwitz
Senior Visual Effects Producer	Nancy St. John

Line Producer	Alton Walpole
Casting by	Tricia Wood, C.S.A. Jennifer Smith, C.S.A. Deborah Aquila, C.S.A.
Unit Production Manager	Alton Walpole
First Assistant Director	Benita Allen
Second Assistant Director	Frederic Roth
Second Assistant Director	Dennis M. Crow
Associate Producer	Marc Sadeghi
Music Supervisor	Dan Hubbert
Stunt Coordinator	John Medlen
Assistant Stunt Coordinator	David Hugghins
Spirit Stunt Double	Ronn Surels
Octopus Stunt Double	Kiante Elam
Sand Serif Stunt Double	Boni Yanagisawa
OS Stunt Double	Tad Griffith
Additional Stunts	Melissa Barker Cayley Bell Thomas DeWier John Cade Michael Hansen Lisa Hoyle Anthony Kramme David Martin Aaron Toney Aaron Walters
Plaster of Paris Choreography by	Joann Jansen
ADR Voice Casting	Barbara Harris
ADR Voices	Catherine Cavadini Peggy Flood Barbara Iley Terence Jay Terence Mathews Jason Pace David Randolph Noreen Reardon Vernon Scott Joel Swetow Andreana Weiner
Production Supervisor	Dawn Todd
Production Coordinator	Elaine K. Thompson
Assistant Production Coordinator	Crystal McAlerney
Production Secretary	Sean Cardinalli
Script Supervisor	Pam Fuller
Camera Operator	Vali Valus
Steadicam Operator	Gregory Lundsgaard
1st Assistant Camera	Greg Luntzel
2nd Assistant Camera	Charlie Newberry
Technocrane Operator	David Hammer
Digital Imaging Technicians	Chad Rivetti Brannon Brown
Digital Loader	Bret Latter
Video Assist	Adam Barth
Production Sound	David J. Brownlow
Boom Operator	Matthew Halbert
Utility Sound	Michael Becker Robert Jerry Brownlow
Key Grip	Anthony T. Mazzucchi
Best Boy Grip	Alexander Griffiths
Dolly Grip	Daniel Pershing
Additional Dolly Grip	Otis Mannick
Grips	Charlie Arnold Matt Debevec Ronald "Pablo" Romero Terry J. Sanchez
Key Rigging Grips	Hank Herrera Gary Kangrga
Best Boy Rigging Grip	Trevor "Zeke" Howe
Rigging Grips	Paul Judges Michael J. Lucero Bryan J. Smith
Chief Lighting Technician	John "Fest" Sandau
Assistant Chief Lighting Technician	Jim "Jimmy C." Cornick
Dimmer Board Operator	Georgia Tays

Set Lighting Technicians	Greg Argarin Jon Caradies Lou Nelson George Rizzo, Jr. John Stearns
Rigging Gaffer	Ray Ortega
Best Boy Rigging Electric	Jason Linebaugh
Rigging Electricians	Frank Garcia Christopher H. Sipes Lucas P. Leggio Louie Martinez Alexander J. Perez
Assistant Art Director	A. Todd Holland
Set Decorator	Gabrielle Petrissans
Leadman	Joel Goodell
Set Dressers	Pierre L. Barrera Benjamin M. Walsh
Buyer	Michael Flowers
On Set Dresser	Bryan DeLara
Key Greens	Christopher Martin
Assistant Greens	Brooke Fair
Art Department Coordinator	John N. Ward
Art Department Production Assistant	Alan Chao
Property Master	Randy Eriksen
Assistant Property Master	Chuck McSorley
Prop Assistant	Brett "Khan" Andrews
Construction Coordinator	Robin Blagg
Construction Foreman	Kirk Newren
Labor Foreman	Albert Rivera
Construction Auditor	Sara Morgan Lewis
Gang Boss	Steve Kahn
Prop Maker / Welder	Brett Cole
Prop Makers	Arthur Arndt Jeff Bolen J. Christie Kenneth Cook Santino Davenport Mark Gutierrez James Herman Andy Linderkamp Jesse McNamara Tony Milhaupt Curtis D. Mott William S. Patterson Jimmy Stephens
Plasterers	Javier Fuentes Dana J. Mestas
Welder	Barton Slade
Utility Techs	Nick Davis Brooke Fair
Key Scenic	Miguel E. Gurulé
Paint Foreman	Nigel Paul Conway
On Set Painter	Dennis Collins
Set Painters	Phillip Brown Daniel Herrera Tim McCullough Sebastian R. Ruiz Katherine Wertz
Assistant Costume Designer	Michael Crow
Costume Supervisor	Richard Schoen
Key Costumer	Frances Vega
Key Set Costumers	Bradford Booth Kathryn Czark
Costumer for Mr. Jackson	Askia Won-Ling Jacob
Costumer	Lora Rael
Costume Buyer	Maureen O'Heron
Tailor	Melissa Moody
Seamstresses	Barbara Lee Brice Olivia Ludi Nancy Molleur
Ager / Dyer / Costumer	Bren Cook
Costume Production Assistant	Lane Stewart
Costume Supervisor (Los Angeles)	Lynda Foote
Costumer (Los Angeles)	Jorge Gonzalez
Ager / Dyer (Los Angeles)	Julia Gombert
Costume Production Assistant (Los Angeles)	Virginia Lise Melin
Make-Up Department Head	Isabel Harkins
Assistant Make-Up Department Head	Art Anthony
Make-up Artist for Mr. Jackson	Allan Apone
Make-up Artist for Ms. Johansson	Heba Thorisdottir
Make-up Artist for Mr. Macht	Melanie Tooker
Make-up Artist for Ms. Mendes	Elaine Offers
Additional Make-up	Bonnie Masoner

Hair Stylist Department Head	Camille Friend
Hair Stylist	Garnett Burk
Hair Stylist for Mr. Jackson	Robert Stevenson
Hair Stylist for Ms. Mendes	Cydney Cornell
Hair Stylist for Ms. Johansson	Barbara Olvera
Additional Hair	John Holland
Special Effects Coordinator	Donald Frazee
Special Effects Foreman	C. Scott Lingard
Special Effects Technicians	Scott Hastings Danny Maldonado Jonathan Delaney Marsh
Make-up Effects	P13 Entertainment, Inc.
P13 Project Coordinator	Anne Kurtzman
P13 Key Sculptor	Gino Crognale
P13 Shop Supervisor	Al Tuskes
P13 Key Prosthetics Applicator	Melanie Tooker
Lifecasts	Gabe Bartalos
Location Manager	Sam Tischler
Assistant Location Manager	S. Reuban Cook
Transportation Captains	N. Marty Radcliff Robert "Bear" Molitor
Driver for Mr. Jackson	Kenny Heath
Driver for Ms. Johansson	Melissa A. Malcom
Driver for Mr. Macht	Alan Mienkes Berger
Driver for Ms. Mendes	Thomas R. Buckley
Drivers	Jason "Jr." Anderson Steve Butler Amber Dawn Cummings Wilson Hayes Michael J. Roybal Gary Shuckahosee Steve Vandiver
Key Office Production Assistant	Armando M. Cruz III Jasmine Mohamed
Office Production Assistants	Dustin DellaVecchia Jason R. Doutree Wendy R. Kennedy Destino Marfil Montez Robert Vertrees Brady Kephart
Assistant to Mr. Jackson	Volney Edward McFarlin III
Assistant to Ms. Johansson	Taryn Cox
Assistant to Mr. Macht	Meredith Engelstein
Assistant to Ms. Mendes	Rowie Green
Assistants to Mr. Miller	Mark DelGallo Emily Cheung Colette Stevens
Assistant to Mr. Walpole	Cayley Bell
Legal Counsel Frank Miller, Inc.	Harris M. Miller II
Second Second Assistant Directors	Brad Arnold Marcia A. Woske
Set Production Assistants	Nick I. Allen J.J. Dalton Julian Duran Ryan Lacen Matt McAlister Randy Rubin Marcus Taylor
Production Accountant	Maeve Mannion
First Assistant Accountants	Beverly L. Jusi Sherrie Bradshaw
Second Assistant Accountant	Nick Cessac
Payroll Accountant	Rich J. Tartaglia
Additional Accountant	Amy Eldridge
Studio Teachers	Kathleen Breton-Collier Amber York
Catering	Reel Chefs Catering / Steve Watson
Chef	Bobby Brual
Chef Assistants	Marco A. Blanco Manny Gonzalez Marciano Moreno Jose Cruz Tejeda Horacio Vazquez
Craft Service	JF Craft & Catering / Joe Fiske
Craft Service Assistant	John Montoya
Set Medics	David Bethel Nicholas Salinas

Unit Publicist	Louise A. Spencer
Unit Still Photographer	Lewis Jacobs
Executive Marketing and Distribution Consultant	Al Newman
Rights & Clearances	Entertainment Clearances, Inc Laura Sevier Cassandra Barbour
Casting Associates (Los Angeles)	Samantha A. Finkler Erin Toner
Casting and Extras Casting (New Mexico)	Gwyn Savage
Casting Assistants (New Mexico)	Valerie McVay Vanessa Vassar
Animal Services Provided by	Boone's Animals For Hollywood
Head Animal Trainer	Ursula Brauner
Animal Trainer	Brian Turi
Undomesticated Quadruped Wrangler	Michael "Puck" Pucker

SECOND UNIT

2nd Unit Director	Stu Maschwitz
Director of Photography	Bobby Finley III
1st Assistant Camera	Chip Byrd
2nd Assistant Camera	Ryan Eustis
Script Supervisor	Lois King
Gaffer	Ray Ortega
Best Boy Electric	Jason Linebaugh
Electricians	Frank Garcia Christopher H. Sipes
Key Grip	Hank Herrera
Best Boy Grip	Trevor "Zeke" Howe
Dolly Grip	Peter Weidenfeller
Grips	Paul Judges Michael J. Lucero Bryan J. Smith
On Set Dresser	Ester Kim
Video Assists	Lance Jay Velazco
Post Production Consulting by EPC	Joe Fineman
Post Production Supervisor	Michael Toji
Post Production Coordinator	Carl Bochek
Post Production Accountant	Bob Weber
Visual Effects Consultant	Bruce Jones
1st Assistant Editor	Stacey S. Clipp
Apprentice Editor	Brad McLaughlin
Visual Effects Editor	A. Ryan Turner
Visual Effects Coordinator	Jonathan O'Brien
Post Production Assistant	Keto Shimizu
Visual Effects by	The Orphanage
Visual Effects Executive Producers	Luke O'Byrne Amy 'Hollywood' Wixson

THE BUNKER CREW

Visual Effects Producer	Kim Doyle
Digital Production Manager	Paul Kolsanoff
Jr. Digital Production Manager	Jaime Norman
Digital Production Coordinator	Daniel Huerta
Digital Production Assistant	Joseph Miller
Associate Visual Effects Supervisor / Colorist	Aaron Rhodes
Post Production Supervisor	Leslie Valentino
Visual Effects Editor	Ivan Landau
Assistant Visual Effects Editors	Anthony Reyna David Fine
On Set Technical Coordinator/ Compositor	Bob Snyder
I/O Operators	Sean Wells Michael Grawert
Lead Concept Artists	Mark Moore Josh Viers Peter Lloyd

THE ORPHANAGE CREW

Visual Effects Supervisor	Rich McBride
Visual Effects Producer	Alex Altrocchi Wolbach
Digital Production Manager	Marny Nahrwold
Production Coordinator	Nichole Wong
Computer Graphics Supervisors	Stephen DeLuca Jon Harman
Animator	Christian Liliedahl
Digital Artist	Sean Murphy
Matte Painter	Thomas Esmeralda
Compositors	Can Chang Kyle McCulloch Youjin Choung Jon Green Heather Abels
Systems Manager	David Lloyd
Systems Engineer	Tim Gross
Manager of Resource Administration	Joe C. D'Amato
Render Wrangler	Brad Isdrab
Set Production Coordinator	Armando Kirwin
Set Production Assistant	Daniel Dinning
Producer	Paul Hettler
Post Production Supervisor	Diane Caliva
Compositing Supervisor	Alex Prichard
Compositors	Kirsten Bradfield Peter Demarest
Storyboard Artist	Mike Kelly
Animator	Webster Colcord
Additional Visual Effects by	Fuel VFX Digital Dimension Riot Entity FX Furious FX Look Effects Inc. Rising Sun Pictures Ollin VFX Cinesoup
Digital Intermediate by	Modern VideoFilm Inc.
Main Title Design by PIC	Pamela Green Florian Bailleul Julio Ferrario Sarah Coatts Jarik van Sluijs
Storyboards drawn by	Frank Miller
Spirit Logo designed by	Steve Miller
Spirit Meat Chart illustration by	Geof Darrow

MUSIC

Supervising Music Editor	Jeff Carson
Score Recorded and Mixed by	Fred Volger
Scoring Assistant	Krystyna Newman
Orchestration	Greg Jamrok
Electronic Programming Assistant	Marty Frasu
Pro Tools Operator	Thomas D. Graham II
Music Preparation	JoAnn Kane Music Service
Vocalist	Diana Newman
Score Recorded at	Newman Stage, Fox Studios
Score Mixed at	M5 Studios, Malibu

"Deutschland Uber Alles"
Performed by Captain Helmut Witten and The German Airforce Band
Written by Joseph Haydn
Courtesy of Legacy International

"Falling in Love Again"
Performed by Christina Aguilera
Produced by Linda Perry
Written by Frederick Hollander and Sammy Lerner
Christina Aguilera appears courtesy of Sony/BMG Music Entertainment